DOS Comma

C000022492

Function

Display information about RAM	
Display the contents of a file	TYPE
Display the disk volume label	VOL
Display the DOS version number	VER
Display the subdirectory structure	TREE
Edit ASCII files	EDIT, EDLIN
Edit DOS line commands	DOSKEY
Edit executable files	DEBUG
Erase a file	DEL, ERASE
Find a character string in a file	FIND
Find files in other subdirectories	APPEND, PATH
Format a blank disk	FORMAT
Get help with DOS	HELP, /?
Install a foreign character set	CHCP, COUNTRY, KEYB, MODE, NLSFUNC, SELECT
Install DOS on hard or floppy disk	FORMAT, SETUP, SYS
List files on a disk or subdirectory	DIR
Load DOS in High Memory Area	DOS
Load programs in memory	DEVICE, DEVICEHIGH, INSTALL, LH, LOADHIGH
Move files to a different subdirectory	COPY, XCOPY, DEL, ERASE
Perform commands conditionally	IF

Computer users are not all alike.
Neither are SYBEX books.

We know our customers have a variety of needs. They've told us so. And because we've listened, we've developed several distinct types of books to meet the needs of each of our customers. What are you looking for in computer help?

If you're looking for the basics, try the **ABC's** series, or for a more visual approach, select **Teach Yourself**.

Mastering and **Understanding** titles offer you a step-by-step introduction, plus an in-depth examination of intermediate-level features, to use as you progress.

Our **Up & Running** series is designed for computer-literate consumers who want a no-nonsense overview of new programs. Just 20 basic lessons, and you're on your way.

SYBEX **Encyclopedias** provide a *comprehensive reference* and explanation of all of the commands, features and functions of the subject software.

Sometimes a subject requires a special treatment that our standard series doesn't provide. So you'll find we have titles like **Advanced Techniques, Handbooks, Tips & Tricks**, and others that are specifically tailored to satisfy a unique need.

You'll find SYBEX publishes a variety of books on every popular software package. Looking for computer help? Help Yourself to SYBEX.

For a complete catalog of our publications:

SYBEX Inc.
2021 Challenger Drive, Alameda, CA 94501
Tel: (415) 523-8233/(800) 227-2346 Telex: 336311
Fax: (415) 523-2373

SYBEX is committed to using natural resources wisely to preserve and improve our environment. This is why we have been printing the text of books like this one on recycled paper since 1982.

This year our use of recycled paper will result in the saving of more than 15,300 trees. We will lower air pollution effluents by 54,000 pounds, save 6,300,000 gallons of water, and reduce landfill by 2,700 cubic yards.

In choosing a SYBEX book you are not only making a choice for the best in skills and information, you are also choosing to enhance the quality of life for all of us.

DOS 5
Instant Reference

DOS® 5
Instant Reference

Robert M. Thomas

SYBEX®

San Francisco • Paris • Düsseldorf • Soest

Acquisitions Editor: Dianne King
Series Editor: James A. Compton
Editors: Ami Knox and David Krassner
Technical Editor: Sheila Dienes
Word Processors: Scott Campbell, Ann Dunn, Lisa Mitchell
Book Designer: Ingrid Owen
Production Artists: Ingrid Owen and Helen Bruno
Screen Graphics: Cuong Le
Desktop Publishing Specialist: M.D. Barrera
Proofreaders: Patsy Owens, Bill Cassel, and Lisa Haden
Indexer: Ted Laux
Cover Designer: Archer Designs

Library of Congress Card Number: 91-65022
ISBN: 0-89588-804-1

Manufactured in the United States of America

10 9 8 7 6 5 4 3 2 1

To Sam Carter of New Braunfels,
who taught me something about writing

Acknowledgments

No individual produces a book. I owe a great debt of gratitude to Ami Knox and David Krassner for their hard work editing the original, unrefined manuscript and assembling its various moving parts into a coherent, consistent whole. Also, many thanks to Dr. Rudolph Langer, who provided his gracious and much-needed support throughout the project, keeping it focused and on track. I am very grateful to Sheila Dienes for her thorough and insightful technical review.

Thanks as well to the following people at Sybex, who made vital contributions and to whom this book, in one way or another, owes its existence: Dianne King, Acquisitions Editor; Barbara Gordon, Managing Editor; Jim Compton, Prompter Series Editor; Scott Campbell, Ann Dunn, and Lisa Mitchell, word processing; Ingrid Owen and Helen Bruno, design and pasteup; M.D. Barrera, type-setting; Patsy Owens, Bill Cassel, and Lisa Haden, proofreading; and Ted Laux, indexer.

Also, many thanks to Microsoft Corporation and Christy Gersich in particular for generously supplying beta versions of the software.

A bit closer to home, I would like to add my heartfelt appreciation for my beloved wife, Krista, for her infinite kindness and patience. Finally, as always, thanks to Roscoe and Elaine, restorers of lost valuable things and keepers of the flame.

B.T.

Table of Contents

Part Three

THE DOS SHELL

Appendix A

USING BATCH FILES

Appendix B

CONFIG.SYS COMMANDS

Appendix C

STANDARD MS-DOS DEVICE DRIVER FILES

Appendix D

GENERAL DOS ERROR MESSAGES

Index

Introduction

DOS 5 Instant Reference is intended for all everyday users of IBM and compatible desktop computers who would like an easy-to-use, practical reference to the productivity tools included in the DOS operating system. Whether you are a novice or experienced user, you will find this book to be a handy source of essential information about the DOS commands. This book also includes basic information on configuring and optimizing your system, plus information on speeding up and simplifying your day-to-day operations using batch files and the new DOS shell. Throughout the book you will find helpful tips on safer and more effective disk file management.

ABOUT DOS VERSION 5.0

Version 5.0 adds a number of important new features that will make DOS more useful and productive for all users, regardless of their level of experience. New 5.0 features include:

- The DOS shell, an optional interface that provides onscreen graphic representation of DOS's file management and application tasks.

- The ability to open more than one application at a time and quickly switch between them, saving time that would otherwise be spent repeatedly opening and closing applications.

- The ability to load most of DOS in the area of RAM above 640Kb. This leaves significantly more memory available for application programs.

- A new, menu-driven text editor that simplifies the process of creating batch files and other ASCII-based system files such as CONFIG.SYS.

- Improved error-recovery features, including the ability to restore deleted files or recover from an accidental disk format.

HOW THIS BOOK IS ORGANIZED

This book covers commands for all versions of DOS through version 5.0, with special emphasis on the new features found in the latest version of the program, and is structured in the following way:

Part 1, "General Rules for Using DOS," provides a brief summary of the common conventions and procedures you need to know to run DOS.

Part 2, "DOS Commands," is an alphabetical listing of all the commands found in DOS; under the heading for each command you will find the following information:

- Each command entry begins with such basic information as whether the command is external or internal, or terminate-and-stay-resident, what versions the command applies to, whether the command will erase or overwrite data, and a brief description of the purpose of the command.

- Syntax lines are given to show how a particular command should be entered at the DOS prompt.

- Practical examples demonstrate proper usage of the command.

- Where applicable, Errorlevel codes and their corresponding meanings are given.

- Error messages that may result from improper usage of a particular command are listed, as well as methods of correcting the problems that arise. (A special appendix lists error messages common to more than one particular command.)

- Instructions for accessing a command through the DOS shell, a special graphic user interface included with version 5.0, appear in the section titled "Using the DOS 5 Shell."

- The "Notes" section that appears near the end of some of the command entries gives special information, warnings, and tips for proper usage of the DOS command under discussion.

- Many command entries end with a list of commands that serve similar or related purposes.

Part 3, "The DOS Shell," describes the unique features of the shell and outlines the necessary procedures for customizing the shell to include any external DOS commands and software initialization commands you care to use.

Special appendixes cover batch files, CONFIG.SYS commands, device driver files, and general DOS error messages.

CONVENTIONS USED IN THIS BOOK

Here is a brief description of the symbols that may appear at the beginning of each command entry:

Note	Meaning
E	The command is an external DOS command.
I	The command is an internal DOS command.
5.0+	The number indicates which versions a command covers. In this example, versions 5.0 and later are covered.
TSR	The command is a terminate-and-stay-resident command.
⊙	The command can erase or overwrite your files, so use with extreme care.

The command syntax lines used in this book employ the following conventions:

- DOS commands appear in uppercase letters, and are followed by a general description of applicable parameters, in the order they must be entered.

- Required command parameters appear without square brackets; optional parameters appear within square brackets.

- Placeholders appear in italic. For example, if *file(s)* shows up in a syntax line, the actual name or names of a file or group of files must be entered.

- The presence of optional command switches is indicated by [*/options*]. If a command allows more than one command switch, they may be combined on the same command line unless otherwise stated.

- All external DOS commands may be preceded by a drive letter and/or subdirectory path indicating the location of the command file on disk. For the sake of simplicity, the examples in this book assume that the subdirectory containing DOS command files is the currently logged subdirectory, or that the subdirectory is part of the operating system's search path.

For example, this is the syntax line for the BACKUP command:

BACKUP *source drive* (\ *path*) (*file(s)*) *target drive* (*/options*)

According to the example, BACKUP requires you to provide parameters for the source drive and the target drive; square brackets indicate that path and file name parameters, as well as optional command switches, can be included, but are not necessary to run BACKUP.

HOW TO USE THIS BOOK

Novice users should begin by reading the next section, "General Rules for Using DOS." Some experienced users may also find it helpful to review the information in that section. All users of version 5.0 should review the information in Part 3, "The DOS Shell." Thereafter, you may use the book on an as-needed basis, to learn the basics of all the commands or just brush up on the features of more familiar commands. Keep the book handy while you work with the computer in case you encounter a strange message or other problem using a command. The aim of this book is to make you more productive and give you the knowledge you need to manipulate your data files with confidence, ease, and safety.

Part 1

General
Rules for Using DOS

The following section describes some of the fundamental concepts that apply to DOS commands and the operating system in general.

ENTERING COMMANDS

Enter DOS commands at the DOS *system prompt,* which is usually a letter on the screen that corresponds to the currently active disk drive. DOS commands are invoked by entering the command *name;* for example, COPY, DIR, or RENAME. Often you may include a number of command *parameters* after the command name. DOS commands and parameters are described in detail in Part 2, "DOS Commands."

The maximum length of a DOS command, including any optional parameters, is 127 characters.

Alternatively, in DOS versions 4.0 and later, you may enter commands using the *DOS shell,* a graphic user interface for the operating system. For details, refer to Part 3, "The DOS Shell."

EXTERNAL COMMANDS

DOS has two types of commands: *external* and *internal.* External commands are actually small, separate utility programs that accompany the operating system and expand its usefulness. If you are using DOS on a floppy-disk system, you will need to insert the DOS diskette containing these programs into your computer's floppy drive before you invoke them.

If you are using DOS on a system with a hard disk, the recommended procedure is to copy all the external program files you intend to use onto a separate subdirectory, such as C:\DOS, and to include this subdirectory name as part of the PATH statement in AUTOEXEC.BAT. If you are unfamiliar with these terms, refer to the PATH entry in this book, or to Appendix A, "Using Batch Files."

If it's necessary to run a DOS external command, you may precede all external commands with a drive letter and/or subdirectory path name to indicate the location of the program file. For example:

A:DISKCOPY A: B:

will run the external DISKCOPY command if the copy of the DISK-COPY command file is on drive A.

C:\DOS\DISKCOPY A: B:

will run the same command if a copy of the command file is in the \DOS subdirectory of drive C.

If the DOS directory is part of the system's PATH statement, or if you are currently logged onto the subdirectory where the DISK-COPY command file resides, you may omit the drive address and command path. For instance:

DISKCOPY A: B:

will run the command under these circumstances. For clarity, the command examples in this book are based on the assumption that you have included your DOS subdirectory in your path statement, or are running DOS from the default drive or subdirectory.

INTERNAL COMMANDS

DOS internal commands are always available to the operator, and may be entered from any DOS prompt. For example:

DIR /P

is an internal command that will execute at any time.

COMMAND HELP

Beginning with version 5.0, all DOS commands accept a special question mark option (**/?**) on the command line. When a command name is followed by this option, DOS does not execute the command, but instead displays a terse description of the particular command's syntax and usage. For example:

COPY /?

returns the following:

Copies one or more files to another location.

Files may also be appended.

COPY (pathname1) (pathname2) (/v) (/a) (/b)

/v Verifies sectors written on the target disk.

/a Copies Ascii files.

/b Copies binary files.

FUNCTION KEYS

DOS provides a limited but handy set of special function keys that assist you when entering repetitive commands or correcting typing mistakes. These keys affect whatever command is currently stored in the *command line buffer,* a portion of RAM used to save and recall the most recently entered command. Only one command at a time (unless you are using a special utility like DOSKEY) is stored in this buffer. (Notice that this buffer is not the same as the *active command line,* which displays command information on the screen as it is entered.) The following list describes these special function keys:

F1 or → (right arrow key)	Enters the first character from the command line buffer on the active command line. DOS remembers its current position within the buffer: if you press F1 again, the next character will appear on the active command line. It is possible to enter the entire contents of the buffer, one character at a time, by repeatedly pressing this key.
F2, then *x*	Enters all the characters from the buffer starting at the current buffer position up to (but not including) the first occurrence of *x*, which is any single character you specify. This is useful for reentering commands in which a single character must be overwritten or added. If the specified character cannot be found in the buffer, this key has no effect.
F3	Enters all the remaining characters in the command buffer, starting from the current cursor position. This key is useful when repeating whole commands with little or no modification.
F4, then *x*	Skips over all the characters in the command line buffer up to the specified character *x*, then enters that character on the command line when you press F1 or →. If you press F3 after entering the character, the remaining portion of the command line buffer is displayed. If the specified character does not appear in the command buffer, this key has no effect.
F5	Replaces the command line buffer with the contents of the active command line. Is also useful for correcting typing errors at the beginning of the command line.

Insert	Switches to Insert mode, whereupon characters you type from the keyboard will be added to the command line buffer at the cursor position, rather than overwriting the character at that position. Press F1, →, or F3 to display the remaining portion of the command line buffer.
Delete	Deletes the character in the current buffer position. This key must be pressed for each character you intend to delete.
Esc	Cancels changes you have made to the command line buffer and restores its original contents. This key must be pressed before you press the Enter key.
Backspace or ← (left arrow key)	Moves cursor to the left one position on the active command line and erases the character at that position. If the erased character was changed from the character in the buffer, the original character in the buffer is restored. If you are already at the beginning of the command line, this key has no effect.

Some application software packages take over the command line buffer for their own purposes, or erase it altogether. If the function keys fail to produce characters on the active command line, it is likely that an application cleared the command line buffer.

Certain key combinations are called *control keys,* because their functions become active when you hold down the control key and type a character. Control keys perform a number of useful services:

Ctrl-C	Stops a DOS command in mid-processing and returns to the DOS prompt.
Ctrl-H	Functions same as Backspace.
Ctrl-P	Causes the console output to be sent to the printer as well as the screen. The printer must be online or the system may cease functioning, at least until the printer is brought online. When the printer is online, pressing this control key a second time will turn the printer echo off.

Ctrl-S   Pauses the execution of the DOS command.
          Useful when large amounts of data flow
          beyond the boundaries of the screen. If your
          keyboard has a Pause key, this key will do the
          same thing. To resume processing, press any
          key (except Ctrl-C or a function key).

Shift-PrtSc   Sends the current contents of the screen to the
               printer.

FILE NAMES

Files are the heart of a DOS system. Related information such as a
letter, book chapter, spreadsheet, database, or application program
is stored under a unique *file name*. A file name is 1–8 characters
long, and may include a *file extension* at the end, which is a period
followed by 3 more characters.

Legal characters in file names include all letters of the alphabet
(upper- and lowercase are treated the same), numeric digits, and
these punctuation marks: **@** ("at" symbol); **#** (number or pound
symbol); **$** (dollar sign); **%** (percent symbol); **^** (caret); **_** (under-
score); and **&** (ampersand).

WILDCARD CHARACTERS

DOS supports two wildcard characters , **?** (question mark) and
* (asterisk), that allow you to specify whole groups of file names.
The **?** stands for any single character in the specified position
within the file name or extension, and the ***** stands for any set of
characters, starting at the specified position within the name or extension and continuing to the end of the file name or extension.

For example, the following syntax describes all files on drive A that have a name beginning with any two characters followed by 001 and any extension:

A:??001.*

The following syntax describes all files on the default drive:

.

REDIRECTING OUTPUT

Many DOS commands display messages of some sort. Normally these messages appear on your monitor screen. However, it is possible to direct the output of DOS commands to another device or to a disk file by means of a *redirection symbol* followed by a *target*.

The redirection symbol for output is the *closing brace*, or *greater-than sign* (**>**).

Standard target device names are as follows:

CON	The console, or screen display (the default)
PRN	The default printing device
LPT1	Parallel printer port #1
LPT2	Parallel printer port #2
COM1	Communications port #1
COM2	Communications port #2
COM3	Communications port #3
COM4	Communications port #4
AUX	An auxiliary output device
NUL	Null device (suppresses output from the command)

In addition to these standard device names, you may redirect output to a file name. If the file that you name does not exist, it is created. If it exists, it will be overwritten. If you want to add to an existing file instead of overwriting it, double the redirection symbol: >>

For example:

DIR > PRN

lists a directory of the current drive and sends the output to the standard printing device.

DIR > DIRFILE.TXT

sends the output to a file named DIRFILE.TXT.

DIR >> DIRFILE.TXT

adds the output from the DIR command to the contents of the file DIRFILE.TXT.

REDIRECTING INPUT

Many DOS commands accept input of one sort or another. Normally, the user enters this input with the keyboard. If the keystrokes that make up this input are capable of being stored in a disk file, DOS can read the file and accept its contents just as if the keystrokes had been typed. This is useful in reducing the margin of error in repetitive tasks. Command input may also be accepted from any device that is capable of supplying data to DOS, such as COM1 through COM4, or AUX.

The redirection symbol for input is the *opening brace,* or *less-than sign* (<).

For example, the MORE command will accept input from a file on disk. The MORE command displays characters on the screen, but if the number of lines of characters is greater than the available screen display, the MORE command pauses and waits for the user to press a key before continuing the display. This prevents characters from scrolling off the screen before the operator has a chance to read them.

MORE < LONGFILE.TXT

displays the contents of LONGFILE.TXT, pausing each time the screen fills.

For another example, consider the CHKDSK/F command, which checks the condition of a data disk. If problems are found, DOS prompts you to enter Y or N to confirm that you would like DOS to fix the problems it found. If you intend always to answer Y, you can create a small text file on disk that contains only the letter Y, followed by Enter. You may call this tiny file Y.TXT. Then, the following command line (which you might place in a batch file) is valid:

CHKDSK/F < Y.TXT

CHKDSK/F, instead of pausing and prompting you for a response, takes the response from the disk file instead.

PIPING

Many DOS commands produce output that can be reprocessed by other DOS commands. One way to do this is to redirect the output to a disk file, and then send the contents of the file as input to the next DOS command.

However, DOS allows a more convenient means of accomplishing this, by permitting you to combine multiple commands on a single command line. This technique is called *piping*, named after the "pipe" character used to combine DOS commands: ¦

The piping technique works as follows: the output of one DOS command is sent to another DOS command, which in turn processes the output it receives, then either sends it to yet another DOS command, or displays the final output. Here are some examples:

CHKDSK /V ¦ MORE

sends the output from the CHKDSK /V command (oftentimes a long list of file names) to the MORE command, which pauses the display of the list each time the screen fills.

CHKDSK C: /V ¦ FIND "COMMAND.COM"

sends the output from the CHKDSK C: /V command to the FIND command, which extracts and displays all occurrences of the file name COMMAND.COM. If you try this command yourself, be sure that you specify the file name entirely in uppercase characters.

DIR C: ¦ SORT ¦ MORE

sends the output of the DIR command to the SORT command, which sorts the file list in alphabetical order, then sends the output to the MORE command, which pauses the display each time the screen fills with file names.

BACKING UP YOUR DATA

This is the prime directive of all computer users; every experienced user knows well to abide by it. Nevertheless, even in this enlightened age, a few unfortunate users will wait until they lose important data before they discover the wisdom of making routine backups.

Computer storage systems hold vast amounts of data that can be wiped out by a technical glitch or careless command entry. If you have current backups of your data, this is usually no more than a temporary annoyance. If you do not have backups, however, it can be an ugly disaster.

Backing up is not difficult, and if you do it regularly, it need not be overly time-consuming. Once you have incorporated a regular system of backing up your data files, the process will fit seamlessly into your daily computing routine. The important thing is to make data backups part of your working habits.

Here's an important tip regarding backups: make them before you experience a problem, not after. If you suddenly discover a problem with your data, there is usually no good purpose in overwriting your current backup disk with another backup; you might replace good data on your backup disk with bad data. If you want to make a copy of your data after you have discovered a problem, do so on a separate set of floppy disks.

You should always have at least one current backup of your data; two backups are preferable. They should be kept in a secure location away from your computer. This will give you the necessary sense of security to experiment with the DOS commands described in this book. Most DOS mistakes will not be destructive; commands with potential to lose data (such as ERASE or COPY) are duly noted in the text.

Part 2

DOS Commands

This section contains a quick reference to all the DOS line commands from versions 1.0 through 5.0, along with examples of their use. Whether you are looking up a particular command or just browsing around, the best way to get a feel for these commands is to read the description of their syntax, then try entering the examples at the DOS prompt. In some cases, you may need to substitute your own system's drive letters, subdirectories, and file names for those used in the examples. Do experiment with variations on the examples you see here, but only after you have made complete, reliable backup copies of your data; that way, if you make a mistake, you can restore data using your backup copy, and try another approach without difficulty.

APPEND

E

3.3+

Establishes a subdirectory search path for data files. When a data search path is set using APPEND, DOS will look in the currently logged subdirectory first, followed by the subdirectories in the search path.

● SYNTAX

First usage:

APPEND /E or /X

Subsequent usage:

APPEND (*source drive*:*path*) (;*additional drive(s)*:*path(s)*) (/*options*)

You may need to invoke APPEND twice: first to set the environment switches (see in the Options section); the second time to specify the subdirectory search path for data files.

Do not attempt to use the /E option (or in version 3.3, the /X option) at the same time you indicate the data search path.

You may name any number of subdirectories in the search path, but you are limited to 127 characters total (including 7 for the APPEND command and a space). Each subdirectory in the search path must be named separately; nested subdirectories are not included automatically. Type a semicolon between each name in the search path.

If you invoke APPEND without parameters, it will display the current data search path.

• OPTIONS

/E   Stores the search path within the DOS environment space, rather than normal RAM. The environment space must be large enough to accommodate the search path; refer to Appendix B, "CONFIG.SYS Commands," for details on adjusting the environment space. This parameter is legal only the first time you invoke APPEND, before you use APPEND again to establish the search path.

/X   (Version 3.3) Allows additional DOS commands (such as COMP or FIND) to access the data search path. Use this parameter only when you first invoke APPEND, before indicating the data file search path.

/X:on   (Versions 4.0+) Allows additional DOS external commands (such as COMP or FIND) to access the data search path. Using /X is the same as using /X:on. You can use this parameter any time when using APPEND.

/X:off   (Versions 4.0+) Cancels the ability of additional DOS external commands (such as COMP or FIND) to use the data search path.

/path:on   (Versions 4.0+) Uses the data search path whether or not data file names include drive letters or subdirectories.

/path:off   (Versions 4.0+) Does not use the data search path if data file names include drive letters or subdirectories.

;   Cancels the current data search path.

• EXAMPLES

APPEND /E/X

places the data search path in the DOS environment space, rather than in normal RAM, and indicates that other commands will use the data search path.

APPEND C:\WORD;\WPDATA

instructs DOS to look for data files on the C:\WORD subdirectory, and the \WPDATA subdirectory on the currently logged drive.

APPEND C:\WORD /path:off

instructs DOS to look for data files on the C:\WORD subdirectory, except for data files that already include a drive letter and/or a subdirectory path name.

APPEND ;

cancels the current data file search path.

● ERROR MESSAGES

APPEND already installed

You have previously invoked APPEND using either the /E or /X option. APPEND may be invoked a second time without these options. To change these options, reboot the computer.

APPEND/ASSIGN conflict

You have attempted to use APPEND after using ASSIGN. Reboot the computer, and load APPEND before using ASSIGN.

● USING THE DOS 5.0 SHELL   You may use APPEND within the DOS shell by selecting the DOS Command Prompt option from the Main Programs window, and then invoking the APPEND command from the DOS prompt. However, because APPEND changes the operating system environment, which is used under these circumstances by a secondary command processor, the subdirectory path information you provide will be discarded, along with the secondary command processor, when you return to the shell using the EXIT command. See the COMMAND entry for details regarding secondary command processors.

● NOTES   Some application software may not be written to take advantage of the data search path. Check that you have designated the search path correctly. Consider using the /X or /X:on parameter

only after you do not get the results you expect with all the commands you would like to use.

APPEND is a natural choice for inclusion in AUTOEXEC.BAT, as it establishes a data search path at boot time.

APPEND works only on data files; use PATH to establish a search path for executable program files. If you intend to use the ASSIGN command, use the APPEND command before you invoke ASSIGN.

See Also   PATH

ASSIGN

E
2.0+

Redirects drive letter references to a second drive letter.

● SYNTAX

ASSIGN *old drive letter = new drive letter* (/Status)

The purpose of the ASSIGN command is to allow older, diskette-based applications software that reference only drives A or B to use hard-disk drives that reference other letters such as C.

You may assign more than one drive letter to another on the same command line.

If you invoke ASSIGN without parameters, DOS resets all drive letters to their original default status. The /Status option displays current changes made with ASSIGN.

• EXAMPLES

ASSIGN A = C B = C

directs all references to drives A and B to drive C instead.

• USING THE DOS 5.0 SHELL
You may use ASSIGN within the DOS shell by selecting the DOS Command Prompt option from the Main Programs window, and then invoking the ASSIGN command from the DOS prompt. However, because ASSIGN changes the operating system environment, which is used under these circumstances by a secondary command processor, it will affect only those applications that you initiate before returning to the shell. When you return to the shell using the EXIT command, the information loaded in memory by ASSIGN will be discarded, along with the secondary command processor. See the COMMAND entry for details regarding secondary command processors.

• NOTES
ASSIGN is intended only for use with old programs that do not reference hard-disk drives. It can cause confusion when used with other DOS commands that accept drive letter parameters or newer application software that can reference any number of disk drives. Do not use ASSIGN unless it is necessary for a particular application software package.

A recommended procedure is to run such applications from a batch file that assigns new drive letters, executes the application, and immediately resets the drive letters when the application terminates.

The FORMAT and DISKCOPY commands in particular do not honor drive redirection.

See Also   SUBST

ATTRIB

E
3.0+

Changes or displays the attributes of a file. Files can be declared read-only, read-write, archived, or not archived. In version 5.0, hidden and system files may also be declared.

● SYNTAX

ATTRIB (*mode option*)(*target drive*:\ *path*\)*file(s)* (/S)

ATTRIB requires a file name parameter. The file name may contain wildcard characters. If called without parameters, ATTRIB will display the attributes of all files matching the indicated file name.

● OPTIONS

/S   Used with file names that contain wildcard characters, or subdirectory names without file names. This option will include matching files in subdirectories nested below the current subdirectory.

You cannot use more than one mode option at a time. The following mode options are used by ATTRIB:

+R   Changes specified file(s) to read-only, which means the file(s) cannot be overwritten or erased

–R   Changes specified file(s) to read-write, which means the files may be overwritten or erased

+A   Changes file setting(s) to Archived

−A   Changes file setting(s) to Not Archived

+H   (Version 5.0+) Changes specified file(s) to hidden, which means the file(s) will not be visible to most DOS operations.

−H   (Version 5.0+) Makes hidden file(s) visible again.

+S   (Version 5.0+) Marks specified file(s) as DOS system file(s).

−S   (Version 5.0+) Removes DOS system-file setting.

• EXAMPLES

ATTRIB ATTRIB.EXE

will display the attributes of the file ATTRIB.EXE.

ATTRIB +R C:\DOS*.* /S

will change all the files on the C:\DOS subdirectory, and any subdirectories nested below \DOS, to read-only.

• USING THE DOS 5.0 SHELL
To change the attributes of files, first select the appropriate files from the file list in the Files display window. Next, select the Files pull-down menu, followed by Change Attributes. A dialog box will appear, indicating the attributes you may change: System, Hidden, Archive, and Read-Only. Any currently active attributes are displayed with a small mark to their left. To change an attribute, highlight it and select it. Pressing the spacebar will toggle the attribute between active and inactive status. When the desired attributes are active, select the OK box, or press Enter.

If you change a file's attribute to Hidden or System, it may no longer appear on the file list. To view such files, select the Options pull-down menu, then select File Display Options. Select the Display Hidden/System Files option, then select the OK box, or press Enter.

• NOTES
Setting a file attribute to read-only is a good way to prevent its accidental erasure. Many files with the extensions .COM

or .EXE can be set to read-only without problems. If you are on a network, you may be required to do this. In some cases, an application's attempt to overwrite a read-only file may generate an error message.

The setting of the Archive bit affects the behavior of other DOS commands. The BACKUP and RESTORE commands will not copy archived files if the /M option is used. XCOPY will only copy archived files if the /A or /M options are used.

BACKUP

| E |

| 2.0+ |

| ⊙ | Can overwrite or erase data!

Copies files from one disk to another in a special format that makes efficient use of disk space.

● SYNTAX

BACKUP *source* (\ *path* \ *file(s))* *target* (/ *options*)

BACKUP requires that you include parameters for a source and a target. The source and target parameters must, at a minimum, specify drive letters. The source drive is the drive holding the files you intend to back up. This is usually a hard-disk drive. The target drive is the location where the backup files will be copied. This is usually a floppy-disk drive.

The target drive and source drive cannot be the same. The target drive must not be changed using the ASSIGN, JOIN, or SUBST commands; in other words, it must be the normal drive letter assigned to the drive at the time the computer was turned on.

You may also include a subdirectory path and file name as part of the source parameter. Wildcard characters are allowed in file names. Other subdirectories that are nested below the specified path may be included if you add the /S option described in the Options section.

● OPTIONS

/A	Adds backup files to the target drive. Does not overwrite existing files on the target drive. The target drive must contain a disk previously created using the BACKUP command.
/D:*mm/dd/yy*	Backs up files that were changed on or after the indicated date.
/F:*size*	(Versions 3.3+) Formats the target disk if ·necessary. FORMAT.EXE (or in some versions, FORMAT.COM) must be in the current directory on the DOS search path for this option to work. This option will not work with removable drives.

(Versions 4.0+) The optional size argument allows you to specify the type of format desired:

160K = 160Kb 5.25", single-sided

180K = 180Kb 5.25", single-sided

320K = 320Kb 5.25", double-sided

360K = 360Kb 5.25", double-sided

720K = 720Kb 3.50", double-sided

1200K or 1.2M = 1.2Mb 5.25", double-sided

1440K or 1.44M = 1.44Mb 5.25", double-sided

/L: *drive:\path\file*	(Versions 3.3+) Writes a separate log file to the source drive, containing the full path name of all backup files, and the number of the target disk to which each was copied.
	Drive:\path\file indicates the exact location and name of the log file. If you specify a drive letter and path name, they must be present and accessible to DOS. The file name must contain only legal characters for file names.
/M	Backs up only those files that were created since the last backup.
/S	Additionally backs up all subdirectories nested beneath the source drive:\path.
/T:*hh:mm:ss*	Backs up files that were altered on or after the indicated time.

• EXAMPLES

\BACKUP C:\ *.* A:

backs up only the files found on the drive C root directory to drive A, and overwrites any files found on drive A before the backup begins.

BACKUP C:\ *.* A: /S /F

backs up all files on drive C (the root directory plus all subdirectories) to drive A. Overwrites all files found on drive A. Formats the disk in drive A if necessary.

BACKUP C:\DOS\ *.* A: /S /A

backs up all files on the drive C DOS subdirectory, plus any subdirectories nested below the DOS subdirectory, to drive A. Adds the backup files it creates to whatever backup files already exist on drive A. The first disk placed in drive A must already contain files previously created with the BACKUP command.

**BACKUP C:*.* A: /S /A /F /D:10-26-91
/L:C:\\DOS\\LOGFILE.OCT**

backs up all the files on drive C that were modified or created after
October 26, 1991, adds them to any backup files already present on
drive A, and formats any disks if necessary. When finished, it
creates the log file c:\dos\logfile.oct. The DOS subdirectory must
already exist to create this file. If the file already exists, BACKUP
will append new data to the end of this file.

● ERRORLEVEL CODES

0 = Normal Completion

1 = No files were found to back up

2 = Some files were not backed up because of errors

3 = BACKUP interrupted by operator's CTRL-C

4 = Premature termination because of errors

● ERROR MESSAGES

Cannot find FORMAT.EXE

You have included the /F option, but DOS cannot locate FOR-
MAT.EXE in order to format a disk. Be sure the directory containing
FORMAT.EXE is on the search path specified with the PATH
command, or else place FORMAT.EXE on the currently logged
subdirectory.

Cannot FORMAT a network drive

You have included the /F option, but the target drive is redirected
over a network. Use a local drive instead.

Cannot FORMAT nonremovable drive

You have included the /F option, but the indicated target is a fixed
disk drive. Use a floppy drive as the target, or else use a previously
formatted fixed disk drive.

Disk full error writing to BACKUP log file

DOS ran out of disk space writing its log file. Cancel with Ctrl-C and restart the command with an empty disk.

Error opening log file

DOS cannot locate the specified backup log file. Check the name and subdirectory location of the file. Correct the syntax and try again. If you did not specify a log file, DOS was unable to open a new log file on the source disk, possibly because the disk was full.

Invalid Date/Time

The date or time specified on the command line was unrecognizable. Correct the entry format and re-invoke the command.

*** Last file not backed up ***

DOS ran out of target disk space attempting to back up the last file, or encountered reading or writing problems with the file or target disk. Copy the file separately to another disk.

No target drive specified

DOS was not able to recognize your target drive specification on the command line, or it was not present. Revise the command line and re-invoke the command.

*** Not able to back up file ***

You have been denied access to the file, usually because you are on a network and the file is currently open, or there are errors in the source file or on the target disk. Try backing up later when the file is closed, or use the /M option to bypass the file. If you suspect source file errors, use the RECOVER command on the source file.

Target cannot be used for BACKUP

Your target disk is too full, or contains errors that make it unsuitable. Use a different disk.

Warning! No files were found to back up

Your source file specification did not match files on disk. Log onto the correct subdirectory, or reenter the command with a different file specification.

● **USING THE DOS 5.0 SHELL**   To back up files from the DOS shell, first select Disk Utilities from the Main Program window, then select Backup Fixed Disk. A dialog box appears, and you may enter the source and destination drives, and any of the options described above. When the source, destination, and options are correct, select the OK box, or press Enter.

● **NOTES**   If the files you intend to back up will not fit onto a single floppy disk, DOS will prompt you to insert another. You must have sufficient disks handy to hold all the files you are backing up. One 5.25" high-density disk stores about 1.2Mb of data. A 5.25" double-sided disk stores a little less than one-third as much. A 3.5" high-density disk stores 1.44Mb; a 3.5" low-density disk stores half as much. You may save some time by having BACKUP format new disks using the /F switch.

Do not mix BACKUP and RESTORE commands from different versions of DOS. Make a note of the DOS version on the backup disk label; always use the same version of DOS to restore files from backup.

You may cancel a back-up procedure using Ctrl-C. You should not attempt to restore files from a backup that was canceled.

As of version 4.0, BACKUP will not back up the DOS system files (COMMAND.COM, IO.SYS, and MSDOS.SYS or IBMBIOS.SYS).

See Also   RESTORE

BREAK

I

2.0+

Determines when the computer checks to see if Ctrl-C, which cancels most DOS commands, was entered by the user.

● SYNTAX

BREAK (ON) (OFF)

BREAK may be invoked with either the ON or OFF parameter. If you invoke BREAK OFF, DOS checks to see if the user entered Ctrl-C during processes that update the screen, write characters to the printer, or read the keyboard buffer. If you invoke BREAK ON, DOS also checks for Ctrl-C during additional functions such as disk reading and writing. More frequent checking for Ctrl-C can cause some slowdown in overall performance during disk reading and writing.

BREAK OFF is the default state when you first boot up.

If you enter BREAK without parameters, DOS reports the current BREAK status.

● EXAMPLES

BREAK ON

most frequently checks for Ctrl-C from the user.

● USING THE DOS 5.0 SHELL   You may use BREAK within the DOS shell by selecting the DOS Command Prompt option from the Main Programs window, and then invoking the BREAK command from the DOS prompt. However, because BREAK changes the operating system environment, which is used under these circumstances by a secondary command processor, it will remain in effect only until you return to the shell using the EXIT command. When you return to the shell, the information loaded in memory by BREAK will be discarded, along with the secondary command processor. See the COMMAND entry for details regarding secondary command processors.

CD OR CHDIR

| I |
| **2.0+** |

Displays or changes the currently logged subdirectory.

● SYNTAX

CD (*source drive:* \ *path*) (..)
CHDIR (*source drive:* \ *path*) (..)

The CD command is a short version of the CHDIR command; they both do the same thing.

If you invoke the CD command with the name of a valid subdirectory on the current drive, DOS logs that subdirectory as the default. If you include a drive letter that is not the current drive, DOS logs the subdirectory on the specified drive as the default, but does not change the currently logged drive and path.

If you invoke CD without options, DOS displays the currently logged subdirectory.

You can log onto a subdirectory that is nested on the next deeper level by invoking CD followed by the subdirectory name.

● OPTIONS

.. Logs to the subdirectory nested just above the current one, if any

• EXAMPLES

The following sequence of commands assumes that you are logged onto drive C, and that drive contains a subdirectory path \DOS\TEXT.

CD C:\DOS\TEXT

logs the \DOS\TEXT subdirectory as the default on drive C.

CD ..

logs onto the \DOS subdirectory, which is one level above \DOS\TEXT.

CD TEXT

logs back down to the \DOS\TEXT subdirectory if you are in the \DOS subdirectory.

CD

displays "C:\DOS\TEXT."

• ERROR MESSAGES

Invalid directory

DOS cannot find the requested directory—it may be nested on another level, or incorrectly entered. Enter the correct subdirectory name. If entered correctly, try moving to the parent or root directory first.

• USING THE DOS 5.0 SHELL   To change to a new default directory, highlight the desired subdirectory in the Directory window, either by scrolling to it using the arrow keys or selecting it with the mouse. This only changes the directory within the shell. When you exit the shell, you will still be in the original directory of entry. Notice that a small "file folder" icon appears to the left of each subdirectory name. A plus sign (+) inside this icon indicates that there

are additional subdirectories nested underneath; selecting the icon will cause the nested subdirectories to appear. If a minus sign (–) appears in the icon, the nested subdirectories are already visible; you may suppress the nested subdirectory display by selecting the icon. If the icon is blank, there are no other subdirectories nested underneath. Press Ctrl-* at any time to force the display of all nested subdirectories.

See Also   MKDIR, MD

CHCP

I

3.3+

Changes or displays the current *code page*, which contains a language-specific character set used by DOS.

● SYNTAX

CHCP (*code page number*)

CHCP may be used to change the current code page by indicating a number corresponding to a valid code page set stored in the system. Here are examples of valid code page numbers:

437	United States
850	Multilingual
860	Portuguese
863	Canadian-French
865	Nordic

CHCP invoked without options displays the currently active code page.

Only one code page may be active at any one time, although you may prepare as many as you need.

● EXAMPLES

CHCP

displays the current code page (437 on most U.S. systems).

CHCP 863

changes the code page to the Canadian-French symbol set, provided that set is prepared for use by your system.

● ERROR MESSAGES

Active code page not available from con device

The desired code page is not valid for the display device you are using. Use a different code page number.

Code page not prepared

You have selected a code page number that has not been prepared fully, if at all. Install NLSFUNC. If you have installed device drivers with your system (using the DEVICE command in CONFIG.SYS), use the MODE CODEPAGE PREPARE command to prepare the desired code page for your device. Then try CHCP again.

Code page operation not supported on this device

You have entered an invalid code page combination, or one that cannot be used on the currently installed device. Check the validity of your code page parameters and re-invoke the command.

Current keyboard does not support this code page

You have entered a code page that is inconsistent with the keyboard's code page. Enter a different code page, or change the keyboard code page using the KEYB command.

● USING THE DOS 5.0 SHELL

You may use CHCP within the DOS shell by selecting the DOS Command Prompt option from the Main Programs window, and then invoking the CHCP command from the DOS prompt. However, because CHCP changes the operating system environment, the selected code page will only remain in effect until you return to the shell using the EXIT command, after which the information loaded in memory by CHCP will be discarded, along with the secondary command processor. See the COMMAND entry for details regarding secondary command processors.

● **NOTES**   Code pages are the means by which DOS supports multiple languages. A code page table defines a set of 256 characters specific to a country or language. The characters are translated from the code page table and displayed on the screen. In order to use an alternate code page, you must first prepare the code page table for use by your system. Details for this process are given in Appendix B, "CONFIG.SYS Commands." Refer also to the commands NLSFUNC and MODE. Once you have prepared code page tables, you may use CHCP to switch between them.

See Also   COUNTRY (Appendix B), NLSFUNC, MODE

CHKDSK

E

1.0+

| ⊙ | Can overwrite or erase data!
|---|

Analyzes, diagnoses, and optionally corrects common hard-disk errors. Reports on the status of files on disk.

● **SYNTAX**

   CHKDSK (*source drive:* \ *path* \ *file(s)*) (/*options*)

If you invoke CHKDSK without parameters, DOS will analyze the current default disk. If you invoke CHKDSK followed by another drive letter, CHKDSK will analyze that drive.

Alternatively, you may specify a file name, including a full sub-directory path if not the currently logged one. Wildcard characters are allowed in file names. In this case, CHKDSK will check the disk and report on whether the specified files are *contiguous* (stored in adjacent areas of the disk) or *noncontiguous* (scattered over separate areas of the disk). Although there is no harm in noncontiguous files, a large number of widely scattered files can noticeably slow down your computer's performance. Several commercial utilities can reorganize noncontiguous files on a hard disk.

● **USING CHKDSK** CHKDSK examines the hard disk and reports certain common errors. The most common errors found by CHKDSK are *lost clusters, cross-linking,* and *allocation errors*.

A lost cluster is an area of disk marked as unusable because it is supposedly occupied by a file, even though DOS can find no file name allocated to that area. Lost clusters normally develop when application programs that write temporary files to disk are interrupted before they can erase these files. Lost clusters are not serious, but they do waste hard-disk space and should be corrected; refer to the /F option in the Options section for details.

Cross-linking occurs when DOS finds more than one file name allocated to the same area of the hard disk. This means that one or all of the files in question are suspect. To correct a cross-linking condition, do the following:

- If the files are data files, back them up onto blank, formatted floppy disks. Do not use any existing backup disks, as you run the risk of overwriting good data with bad. Examine the files on the floppy disk to determine which ones are damaged. Erase the files on the hard disk and, if possible, replace them with verified backups.

- If any of the cross-linked files are executable program files, erase them and replace them using your master backup disks. Do not simply copy the backup files onto the hard disk, as this may not alleviate the cross-linked condition. Erase the files on the hard disk first, then copy the backups.

File allocation errors occur when the record of hard-disk space allocated to the files is inconsistent, impossible, or unreadable for any reason. CHKDSK will attempt to correct the problem if you have specified the /F option, but it may not be able to do so. If a file is damaged because of allocation errors, erase it and replace it from your backup disk.

After damaged files are replaced, run CHKDSK again to verify that the problem is solved.

Cross-linking and file allocation errors can be temporary problems (the result of power surges and spikes, for example) or they can be symptoms of more serious hardware problems. If these problems persist, have your computer checked by a qualified service technician.

● OPTIONS

/F   Enables auto-correction mechanism. When lost clusters are found, this message is displayed:

> **nn lost clusters found in n chains**
> **Convert lost clusters to files (Y/N)?**

where *n* is a number indicating the quantities involved. If you answer Y, the lost clusters are converted to files with the extension .CHK on the root directory. If you answer N, the lost clusters are simply removed. In versions prior to 5.0, if you have not specified the /F option, this message will still appear, but answering it has no effect.

/V   Displays the name of each file on disk as it checks. Because hard disks can contain hundreds of files, this option will often produce a long report. You may wish to redirect the report to a file.

● EXAMPLES

CHKDSK /F

checks the current hard disk and attempts to fix any errors it finds.

CHKDSK D:\DOS\ *.* /V > D:\STATUS.FIL

checks the files on the D:\DOS subdirectory, displays the name of all the files on disk, and redirects the output to a file named D:\STATUS.FIL.

● ERROR MESSAGES

Allocation error, size adjusted

There is a discrepancy between the size of the file on disk and that reported in the file allocation table (FAT). If you have specified the /F option, CHKDSK revises the file allocation table automatically.

Cannot CHKDSK a network drive

Do not attempt to use CHKDSK over a network.

Cannot CHDIR to path

CHKDSK cannot verify the existence of a subdirectory reported in the FAT. Run CHKDSK with the /F option to correct the problem.

Cannot CHDIR to root

CHKDSK cannot locate the start of the root directory. Reboot the computer and re-invoke the command. If the problem continues, back up what files you can, if any, and reformat the disk.

Cannot CHKDSK a SUBSTed or ASSIGNed drive

Cancel drive assignments made with SUBST or ASSIGN and run CHKDSK again.

Cannot recover entry

CHKDSK has found subdirectory errors. If you have specified the /F option, CHKDSK will attempt to correct them automatically. Otherwise, the disk is unusable and should be reformatted or discarded.

Convert directory to file?

The subdirectory contains too many errors to recover. You may answer Y to this question to convert it to a file, review the contents, and possibly recover some data.

Convert lost chains to files?

CHKDSK has discovered lost chains, which are areas of the disk that include data not assigned to files in the FAT. Answer Y to this question if you would like to recover this disk space. CHKDSK will convert the lost chains to files, giving them the name FILE*nnnn*.CHK, where *nnnn* is a number from 0000 to 9999. You can review, edit, rename, or delete these files as you wish.

Corrections will not be written to disk

CHKDSK has found errors, but makes no attempt to repair them. Re-invoke the command using the /F option.

Directory is joined

CHKDSK bypasses directories that have been joined to other drives. Invoke the JOIN command with the /D option, and re-invoke CHKDSK.

.. Does not exist

The current or parent directory is invalid. If CHKDSK stops processing, reboot the computer and re-invoke the command.

Entry has bad attribute

CHKDSK has discovered an invalid subdirectory entry. If you have specified the /F option, CHKDSK will try to correct the problem.

(*file*) is cross-linked on allocation unit

CHKDSK has found two files that share the same area of the disk. If you have specified the /F option, the named file is truncated to remove the discrepancy.

Invalid allocation unit, entry truncated

The FAT is indicating an invalid disk location for a file. If you specified the /F parameter, the file size is changed to zero bytes and the data is lost.

Insufficient room in root directory

CHKDSK has run out of room in the root directory for storing its recovered files (FILE*nnnn*.CHK). Review, backup, and delete the recovered files as needed to make more room, and re-invoke CHKDSK.

Non-DOS disk Continue?

CHKDSK does not recognize the format of the disk. If you answer Y to this prompt and CHKDSK cannot correct the problem, reformat the disk.

Processing cannot continue

CHKDSK has run out of available RAM; this can happen when using very large disks. Obtain more memory before running CHKDSK on this disk.

● **USING THE DOS 5.0 SHELL** You may run the CHKDSK command from the DOS shell by selecting the DOS Command Prompt option from the Main Programs window, and then entering the CHKDSK command at the DOS prompt. To return to the shell, invoke the EXIT command.

● **NOTES** Because CHKDSK's automatic error-correction mechanism can overwrite information you may not want to lose, it is advisable to run it twice: the first time without the /F option to determine if cross-linking or allocation errors exist that would be better to correct manually, and the second time with the /F option to automatically erase lost clusters or fix other errors.

If you redirect CHKDSK's disk status report to a file, any message regarding lost clusters will go to the file also. If you have redirected CHKDSK's output and it seems to have paused for an unusually long time, try typing Y followed by Enter.

Do not attempt to use CHKDSK across a network. Do not use CHKDSK on drives that have been renamed with the ASSIGN, JOIN, or SUBST commands.

CLS

I
2.0+

Clears the screen.

● SYNTAX

CLS

The CLS command is invoked without parameters. It will erase all characters on the screen and display the operating system prompt, if any, on the first line of the display.

● **USING THE DOS 5.0 SHELL**   CLS is not intended for use within the DOS Shell. It functions either at the DOS command prompt, or within batch files.

● **NOTES**   If your display is configured for more than 25 lines, CLS may not clear it properly. Check the documentation for your display device for alternatives to CLS.

COMMAND

E
1.0+

Invokes a secondary command processor. Secondary command processors are normally used by application software to create a new DOS environment (called a *shell*) while the original application is still running, for purposes of executing file management commands or additional applications. In versions of DOS prior to 3.3, COMMAND was used to execute batch files from within other batch files, and then return to the original upon completion.

● SYNTAX

COMMAND *(source drive:\path)* *(device)* *(options)*

COMMAND called without parameters starts a new command processor. A secondary command processor is loaded as a copy of the parent processor, and includes the parent processor's environment settings. If you change settings in the secondary processor, they are lost when you return to the parent processor. To return to the parent processor, invoke the EXIT command.

You can nest additional secondary processors, but available RAM is reduced slightly for each one.

If you include the source drive and path parameters, the new command processor will look for the file COMMAND.COM on that subdirectory as needed; otherwise it looks for COMMAND.COM in the same location as the primary processor.

In versions 4.0+, you may specify an auxiliary device parameter (such as COM1, for connection to a remote terminal). The effect of this parameter is the same as invoking the CTTY command in the secondary processor.

● OPTIONS

/E:*nnnnn*   Creates a new environment size for
                       variables. (See the SET entry for details
                       regarding DOS variables.) The range
                       for a valid environment size is 160 to
                       32,768 bytes.

/P   Allows the secondary command processor to function as the primary
processor. DOS will not automatically
return to the parent processor, but
instead requires that the EXIT
command be explicitly invoked.

/C *command string*   Invokes a DOS command or executable
file and returns to the parent processor
immediately upon completion (unless
the /P switch has also been invoked).

/MSG   (Version 5.0+) Loads all DOS error
messages into memory. Use this option
when running DOS on a floppy-disk
based system where you are switching
disks frequently. You must use the /P
option with this option.

● EXAMPLES

COMMAND

loads the secondary processor and displays the current version
of DOS.

COMMAND /P /E:1024

loads the secondary processor, indicates that it is to be treated as the
primary processor, and enlarges the DOS environment space to
1024 bytes. This is the only way to enlarge the environment size in
DOS versions prior to 3.3.

COMMAND /C MY-PROG

loads the secondary processor, executes the batch file MY-
PROG.BAT, and returns to the parent processor at the conclusion of
MY-PROG. In DOS versions prior to 3.3, this is the only method for
calling an additional batch file from within a batch file, and then
returning to the original batch file afterwards. Although commonly
used with batch files, this syntax will function the same way for any
executable file.

• ERROR MESSAGES

Invalid environment size

You entered an invalid number of bytes with the /E option. Enter a size between 160 and 32,768 bytes.

• USING THE DOS 5.0 SHELL
To load a secondary processor with the DOS Shell, select the DOS Command Prompt option from the Main Programs window. To return to the shell, invoke the EXIT command at the DOS prompt.

• NOTES
Do not load TSR (terminate-and-stay-resident) programs, such as SIDEKICK, or run any program that makes lasting changes to the organization of RAM, while within a secondary processor. These types of programs may cause unpredictable results when you return to the parent processor, and may lead to the loss of data. Especially avoid loading such programs from within application software (spreadsheets, word processors, and so on) that allows you to access the DOS prompt without leaving the program. TSR programs installed in this manner can conflict with the application's organization of RAM. If you intend to use a TSR program, load it while in the primary processor, then create the secondary processor.

See Also   EXIT, CALL

COMP

E

1.0+

Tests two files to determine if their contents are identical.

• SYNTAX

COMP (*drive*:\ *path* \ *file(s)*) (*drive*:\ *path* \ *file(s)*)

If you invoke COMP without parameters, DOS will prompt you for the names of the file sets to compare. The rules for responding to the prompts are the same as those for entering parameters.

COMP requires, at a minimum, the names of two files. You may include wildcard characters in the file names for comparison. If you do so, DOS compares the files that match each other within the naming convention represented by the wildcard characters.

• USING COMP   COMP will compare the contents of the files you specify on a byte-to-byte basis. If the files are identical, DOS responds with this message:

Files compare OK

In versions before 4.0, if the files are not the same size, DOS reports this and does not compare their contents. In versions 4.0+, DOS reports the size difference and then prompts:

Do you wish to continue (Y/N)?

If you answer by entering Y, DOS compares the files.

As COMP compares files, if it finds that bytes in the same position in the files are not equal, the following message appears:

Compare error at OFFSET *x*
file1 = *nn*
file2 = *nn*

where *x* is the position of the bytes within each file, and *nn* is the hexadecimal representation of the unequal number of bytes found. Upon reaching the end of the files, or after finding 10 such inequalities, DOS ends the comparison process.

• OPTIONS

/A   (Version 5.0) Displays differences in ASCII format.

/C   (Version 5.0) Causes COMP to ignore the case of letters.

/D   (Version 5.0) Displays differences in decimal format. This switch will override the / A switch on the command line.

/L   (Version 5.0) Includes the line number instead of file offset. This is the default state for text files. It need be specified only when comparing binary files that have line numbers.

/N:*nnn*   (Version 5.0) Indicates a maximum number of lines to compare, starting at the beginning of each file, where *nnn* is the indicated maximum.

● EXAMPLES

COMP *.* *.BAK

compares all files on the currently logged drive and subdirectory with all files of the same name having a .BAK extension.

COMP C: A:

compares all files on the currently logged subdirectory of drive C with files of the same name on the currently logged subdirectory of drive A.

COMP C:\AUTOEXEC.BAT C:\AUTOEXEC.OLD

compares AUTOEXEC.BAT on the root directory of drive C with AUTOEXEC.OLD in the same location.

● ERROR MESSAGES

Files are different sizes

COMP cannot compare two files that are not the same size.

10 mismatches - ending compare

COMP automatically stops processing after 10 mismatches.

● **USING THE DOS 5.0 SHELL** You may run the COMP command from the shell by selecting the DOS Command Prompt option from the Main Programs window, and entering the COMP command at the DOS prompt. To return to the shell, invoke the EXIT command. Refer to Part 3, "The DOS Shell," for details about adding this and other commands to the program window within the shell.

● **NOTES** If a file does not end with Ctrl-Z (the end-of-file marker), COMP returns this message:

EOF marker not found

This message may be displayed even when files are identical. Since many files do not end with this character, this message is purely informational and does not relate to the comparison or integrity of the compared files.

See Also DISKCOMP

COPY

| I |

| 1.0+ |

| ⊙ | Can overwrite or erase data!

Copies and combines files.

● **SYNTAX**

COPY source (drive:\path\) file(s) (target drive:\path\file(s)) (/options)

Alternative syntax for combining files:

COPY *source file(s)+source file(s)* (*+source file(s)+ ...*)
target (*drive:\path\file(s)*)

At a minimum, the COPY command requires a *source file name*, which may include wildcard characters, plus optional drive letter and subdirectory path. Optionally you may provide a target parameter, which may be another file name, drive letter, or subdirectory path, or a combination of the three. If you do not include a target, COPY will attempt to copy the source files onto the currently logged drive and subdirectory.

The source and target may not indicate the same file name in the same location. In other words, the COPY command will not copy a file onto itself.

If the target is a drive and/or a subdirectory but does not include a file name, a copy with the same name as the source file is made in the target location. If you indicate subdirectories, they must be preceded by a backslash (\) character.

If you use wildcard characters to indicate multiple source files and the target does not include a file name, a set of individual copies of each file matching the source specification will be made in the target location.

If you indicate multiple source files and the target file name also includes wildcard characters, DOS will attempt to rename the target files in accordance with the wildcard conventions that you indicate. For predictable results, keep the wildcard character specifications consistent between the source and target file names.

If you indicate multiple source files and the target is a single file name, DOS will combine the source files matching the wildcard specification into the single target file.

Alternatively, you may combine files by listing source files, separating them with a plus sign (+). These source files may include wildcard characters as well. The files will be combined into the file you indicate as the target file. It is inadvisable to combine files if one of the source files has the same name as the target. However, you may omit a target file name, and DOS will combine the source files into a file with the same name as the first source file, thereby over-writing it.

● OPTIONS

/A   Indicates that the files are to be treated as ASCII files. The location of this switch in the command line is important. It affects the file name immediately preceding it, plus all file names that follow it until another /A or /B switch is encountered. When a file is treated as an ASCII file, it is read until a Ctrl-Z (end-of-file) character is encountered, or until DOS has read the maximum number of bytes as specified in the file directory. If this switch is used after the target file name, a Ctrl-Z character will be added to the end of the target file.

/B   Indicates that the files are to be treated as binary files. As with the /A switch, the location of this switch in the command line is important. It affects the file name immediately preceding it, plus all file names that follow it until another /A or /B switch is encountered. When a file is treated as a binary file, DOS will continue reading when a Ctrl-Z character is encountered, to the reported size of the file. If this switch is used after the target file name, a Ctrl-Z character will not be added to the end of the target file.

/V   Instructs DOS to perform a validity check on the target files after they are created. The extra step of verification will slow COPY down slightly. The same effect can be made default with the command VERIFY ON.

● EXAMPLES

COPY /B *.* A:

copies all files on the currently logged drive and subdirectory to drive A. DOS ignores end-of-file characters. Remember to include the colon after the drive letter. If you forget, all the files on the currently logged drive and subdirectory will be copied into one file named A.

COPY /A *.TXT *.BAK /A /V

copies all files with extension .TXT to files with the same name and extension .BAK. DOS honors end-of-file characters in all files, appends an end-of-file character on each new file it creates, and verifies the copies that are made.

COPY /B *.TXT \BACKUP /V

copies all files with extension .TXT to a subdirectory named BACKUP on the same logged drive. All files are treated as binary files, and DOS verifies the copies that are made.

COPY A:*.TXT

copies all files on drive A with the extension .TXT to the currently logged drive and subdirectory. The currently logged drive must not be drive A.

COPY START.FIL + MIDDLE.FIL + END.FIL COMPLETE.FIL

combines START.FIL, MIDDLE.FIL, and END.FIL into one file called COMPLETE.FIL.

COPY REPORT.TXT + *.TXT

copies all files with extension .TXT, except REPORT.TXT, into REPORT.TXT. DOS honors REPORT.TXT as the target file name because it is the first name on the list of files to combine. However, notice that the wildcard specification, *.TXT, would include REPORT.TXT. DOS cannot honor the instruction to combine REPORT.TXT with itself, and thus the contents of REPORT.TXT are not duplicated in the resulting file.

COPY /A LETTER.TXT PRN

copies a file to the standard printing device. Be sure your printing device is online, or DOS will simply wait, not accepting any further input. In addition to PRN, you may also copy files to the device names COM1, COM2, COM3, COM4, AUX, CON, LPT1, or LPT2. Not all systems support all of these device names. If your system does not support the device name, DOS will create a disk file with that name.

• ERROR MESSAGES

Cannot do binary reads from a device

Do not specify the /B option under these circumstances. If necessary, use the /A option to force an ASCII copy.

Content of destination lost before copy

The source file was overwritten before the copy process could be completed. Restore the source file from backup, and re-invoke the COPY command using correct syntax.

File cannot be copied onto itself

You have specified the same file as both the source and the target. This is usually done when using wildcard characters in the file specification. Correct the syntax and try again.

• USING THE DOS 5.0 SHELL
To copy files, first select the desired files from the list in the File List window. Then press the F8 key, or select the Files pull-down menu, followed by Copy. A dialog box will appear, indicating the chosen file(s) and the new destination. To change the currently displayed destination, type a new one. If you would like to edit the current destination, press the right or left arrow key before typing any characters. If you wish to change the source listing, press Esc or select CANCEL and choose different files from the display window.

When you have entered the desired destination, press Enter or select the OK box, and the files will be copied.

• NOTES
The /A switch, which adds an end-of-file marker to the destination file, is designed for special circumstances in which some older applications may require an end-of-file marker in files that they read.

The /B switch is designed for circumstances in which binary information may be lost or misinterpreted; for example, if you are using the COPY command to send downloadable soft fonts to your printer.

The /V switch compares the contents of the target file on a sector-by-sector basis to an image of the file in RAM, not to the actual source file on disk. Thus, this switch will detect errors writing the target file, but can miss errors that may occur reading the source file into RAM.

For everyday purposes of making copies of files on disk, most files will copy just fine without the use of any of COPY's optional switches. The general rule is this: If you don't really need them, don't use them.

See Also   XCOPY

CTTY

```
| I |
|2.0+|
```

Redirects console input and output to a named hardware device. When console input and output is redirected, the computer can operate on instructions and display messages using a remote input/output device.

● SYNTAX

CTTY *device name*

CTTY requires a valid hardware device name. Common secondary device names include COM1, COM2, COM3, and COM4, which specify communications ports, or AUX, which would indicate another terminal connected to the computer.

● EXAMPLES

CTTY COM1

instructs DOS to handle subsequent input and output through the COM1 communications port.

CTTY CON

redirects input and output functions through the default device (usually the keyboard and monitor). This command must be sent from whatever input device is current, for example, a remote terminal connected via a *COM* port.

● USING THE DOS 5.0 SHELL
You may invoke CTTY from the DOS shell by selecting the DOS Command Prompt option and invoking the command from the DOS prompt. The redirected input/output device must invoke the EXIT command to return to the shell. When used this way, CTTY can cause unpredictable results in the shell, especially if you are using a mouse. Do not use CTTY within the shell unless you are an expert regarding DOS I/O functions.

● NOTES
Applications that do not use DOS for input and output (that is, they have their own internal instructions for sending and receiving data) will not honor any redirection made using CTTY.

Even if you redirect input and output using CTTY, you can still reboot the computer with Ctrl-Alt-Del from the default system keyboard.

See Also MODE

DATE

1.1+

Displays or sets the system date.

● SYNTAX

DATE (*date*)

If you invoke the DATE command without parameters, DOS displays the current system date and prompts you to enter another. Dates are accepted using the format *mm/dd/yy*, where *mm* is the month (1–12), *dd* is the day (1–31), and *yy* is the year from 1980 to 2079 (80–79).

Some alternate formats are accepted. You may use hyphens (-) rather than slashes (/) to separate the month, day, and year. You may also use 4 digits for the year (1980–2079).

Date formats used in other countries are accepted if you have changed the code page to another character set, using the COUNTRY command in CONFIG.SYS. See Appendix B, "CONFIG.SYS Commands," for details.

If you include the date in an accepted format on the command line, DOS changes the date without displaying a message.

● EXAMPLES

DATE

displays the current date and prompts you to enter another. To leave the date unchanged, press Enter.

DATE 10-26-91

changes the date to October 26, 1991.

● ERROR MESSAGES

Invalid date

DOS cannot recognize the date format you have entered, or you have entered a nonexistent date. Check your entry and try again.

● **USING THE DOS 5.0 SHELL**   You may display or change the current date by selecting the DOS Command Prompt option from the Main Programs window, and entering DATE at the DOS prompt. To return to the DOS shell, invoke the EXIT command.

● **NOTES**   DOS maintains a system date even if your computer does not have an internal clock.

If your computer has an internal clock, the DATE command in DOS versions 3.3 and earlier will not reset it. You must use a separate utility program, usually supplied by the manufacturer, to reset the internal clock mechanism. As of version 3.3, if DOS can read your computer's internal clock, the DATE command will reset it.

If you do not use an AUTOEXEC.BAT file, DOS invokes the DATE command automatically at startup. If you are using AUTOEXEC.BAT, you must include the DATE command in the file to achieve the same effect.

See Also   TIME

DEL OR ERASE

   Can erase data!

Deletes files.

● SYNTAX

DEL (*drive:* \ *path* \ ) *file(s)* (/ *options*)
ERASE (*drive:* \ *path* \ ) *file(s)* (/ *options*)

The DEL and ERASE commands function identically. All references in this section to the DEL command apply as well to the ERASE command.

DEL requires that you specify the name of a file to delete. Wildcard characters may be used to erase groups of files. You may also specify a drive letter and subdirectory path, if different from the currently logged path.

If you use the wildcard specification *.*, meaning all the files on the current subdirectory, DOS prompts

Are you sure?

If you really intend to delete all the files, enter Y in response to this prompt. If you enter N, the command is canceled.

● OPTIONS

/P (Versions 4.0+) Instructs DOS to display each file that matches the file name parameter and prompt, "Delete (Y/N)?" If you enter Y, the file is deleted. If you enter N, the file is left alone. This safety device can help prevent you from accidentally deleting files. It also allows you to selectively delete files from a group.

● EXAMPLES

DEL EXAMPLE.TXT

deletes the file EXAMPLE.TXT.

DEL *.BAK

deletes all files on the current subdirectory with the extension .BAK.

DEL A:*.BAK

deletes all files on drive A with the extension .BAK.

DEL C:\BACKUP*.BAK /P

displays each file on the C:\BACKUP subdirectory with the extension .BAK, and prompts for confirmation before deleting it. To confirm, enter Y.

● **USING THE DOS 5.0 SHELL**   To delete files, select the desired files in the File List window, and then press the Delete key. Alternatively, after selecting the desired files, you may then select the Files pull-down menu, followed by Delete. A dialog box then appears, asking you to confirm that you really want to delete the selected files. Press Enter or select the OK box and the files are deleted. If you change your mind, press Esc or select the Cancel box.

● **NOTES**   Prior to version 5.0, DOS provided no mechanism for recovering a file once it had been deleted. However, several software manufacturers have developed commercial utilities to accomplish this task. DOS version 5.0 includes one such utility, UNDELETE.EXE. See the UNDELETE entry for details.

If you must recover a file that has been accidentally deleted, do so as quickly as you can. If possible, do not use the computer for any other operation until any accidentally deleted files have been recovered.

See Also   UNDELETE

DELOLDOS

E

Can overwrite or erase data!

Removes old DOS files after installing version 5.0.

● SYNTAX

DELOLDOS /*options*

Use the DELOLDOS command to recover space on your hard disk that is occupied by copies of the previous version's DOS files that were saved by the DOS 5.0 SETUP command. After you have run DELOLDOS, you will not be able to use the Uninstall disk to restore your previous DOS version.

DELOLDOS displays full-screen menus and prompts that direct you to confirm that you want to delete the old DOS files and offer step-by-step instructions for the process. If you installed DOS on floppy diskettes, have those diskettes handy.

● OPTIONS

/B   Forces a black-and-white menu display on color monitors, or monochrome monitors that cannot support the default color display.

● EXAMPLES

DELOLDOS /B

runs the DELOLDOS program in black-and-white.

DIR

Displays a list of files in a directory.

● SYNTAX

DIR (*drive***:\ ***path***\ ***file(s)***) (/ ***options***)**

If you invoke DIR without parameters, it will display a list of files in the currently logged drive and subdirectory.

You may specify a drive or subdirectory other than the current one by specifying it on the command line.

You may limit the files included in the directory list by indicating a file name. If the file name contains wildcard characters, only those files that match the specification will be included.

Unless you specify the /W option, DOS displays the list one file to a line, including the file name, extension, size in bytes, date, and time the file was created.

● OPTIONS

/P   Causes the list of files to pause each time the file list fills the screen during the display. Press any key to continue displaying files in this manner, until DOS reaches the end of the list.

/W   Causes only file names and extensions to be listed, in a wide format with as many as five file names per line

/S	Displays files in all subdirectories nested below the specified directory
/B	Displays file and directory names only
/L	Displays file names in lowercase (mimics UNIX)
/O:*order*	List files in sorted order, where *order* is a letter indicating the one of the following:

> N = File name, then by extension
>
> S = File size
>
> E = File extension, then by name
>
> D = Chronological order
>
> G = Group files by subdirectories

To reverse the selected order, place a hyphen (-) before the *order* parameter.

/A:*attrib*	Includes only those files with specified attributes, where *attrib* is a letter indicating the type of attribute to include in the listing:

> A = Files with archive bit set
>
> D = Subdirectories only
>
> R = Files marked read-only
>
> H = Hidden files
>
> S = System files

To reverse the meaning of the attribute, precede the *attrib* letter with a hyphen (-); for example, -A would indicate "files without the archive bit set."

● EXAMPLES

DIR A:

lists all the files on drive A.

DIR C: /P/W

lists all the files on the currently logged subdirectory of drive C, in wide format (names only), and pauses the display each time the screen fills up with file names.

DIR /O:N /A:H

displays only hidden files in alphabetical order.

● ERROR MESSAGES

Error occurred in environment variable

The DIR command syntax stored in the DIRCMD environment variable is incorrect. Correct the contents of the DIRCMD variable using the SET DIRCMD= command.

● USING THE DOS 5.0 SHELL   To display the files in a sub-directory, highlight the directory in the Directory Tree window, and the files in that directory will be displayed in the File List window. You may display the files in two directories simultaneously by selecting the View pull-down menu, followed by the Dual File Lists option. This will force a second directory display to appear below the first. You may move among the displayed windows using either the mouse or the Tab key, which will activate each window in sequence. To view hidden files, select the Options pull-down menu, then select File Display Options. Select the Display Hidden/System Files option. Finally, select the OK box or press Enter.

● NOTES   You may store a default set of DIR command switches in the DIRCMD environment variable. For example:

SET DIRCMD=/O:N

indicates that all future DIR command calls will be in alphabetical order by file name. If you would like to override the DIRCMD switch temporarily, include the parameter on the command line, preceded by a hyphen (-). For example:

DIR /O:-N

would override the example DIRCMD switch.

DISKCOMP

| **E** |
| **1.1+** |

Compares the contents of two floppy disks on a track-by-track basis, reporting which track numbers are not identical.

● SYNTAX

DISKCOMP *source drive*: (*second drive:*) (*/options*)

DISKCOMP requires that you enter a source drive. This drive must be a drive letter for a floppy-disk drive.

If you do not specify a second drive for comparison, DOS uses the current default drive for the second drive.

If the source drive and the second drive are the same, DOS first reads the floppy disk in the source drive, then prompts you to remove the disks and insert the second disk into the same drive. You may have to switch disks more than once to complete the comparison process.

● OPTIONS

/1   Instructs DISKCOMP to compare only the first side of each disk, even double-sided disks.

/8   Instructs DISKCOMP to compare only the first 8 sectors of each track, even if the tracks have 9 or 15 sectors.

● EXAMPLES

DISKCOMP A:

compares the disk in drive A with the disk in the currently logged drive. If the current drive is drive A, DISKCOMP prompts you to switch disks at various times during the comparison.

DISKCOMP A: B: /1/8

compares the disk in drive A with the disk in drive B. Compares only the first side of each disk, and only the first 8 sectors of each track.

● ERRORLEVEL CODES

0 = Disks are identical

1 = Disks are not identical

2 = Operator interrupted comparison with Ctrl-C

3 = Comparison interrupted by data errors or damaged disks

4 = Invalid drive letters, drive types, or syntax error

● ERROR MESSAGES

Cannot DISKCOMP to or from an ASSIGNed or SUBSTed drive

One of the drives your are attempting to compare is assigned using the ASSIGN or SUBST command. Remove the assignments before re-invoking the DISKCOMP command.

Cannot DISKCOMP to or from a network drive

Do not attempt to invoke DISKCOMP on a drive that has been redirected over a network.

Compare process ended

The DISKCOMP process ended early because of disk read errors, such as bad sectors or file allocations. Run the CHKDSK command on the disks to analyze the problem and correct it if possible.

Do not specify filename(s)

Do not include file names with drive types when invoking the DISKCOMP command. Correct the syntax and try again.

Drive or diskette types not compatible

You have attempted to use the DISKCOMP command on drives with two different format types. Use the COMP or FC command instead.

Diskette bad or incompatible

One of the disks has an incorrect format, is copy-protected, or contains data errors. If the disk is not copy-protected, use the CHKDSK command to attempt to correct the problems.

Specified drive does not exist, or is non-removable

You have invoked the DISKCOMP command using a fixed disk drive, or an invalid drive letter. DISKCOMP is intended for use on floppy disks only. Correct the syntax and try again.

● **USING THE DOS 5.0 SHELL**   You may use DISKCOMP within the DOS shell by selecting the DOS Command Prompt option from the Main Programs window, and invoking the DISKCOMP command from the DOS prompt. To return to the shell, invoke the EXIT command.

● **NOTES**   DISKCOMP will only compare floppy disks that are the same size and data density. For example, you cannot compare a 5.25", 1.2Mb disk with a 5.25", 360Kb disk. You cannot compare hard disks or RAM disks using DISKCOMP.

You cannot use DISKCOMP on drives that have been reassigned using the ASSIGN, JOIN, or SUBST commands. You cannot use DISKCOMP to compare drives across a network.

You can compare the contents of different drive types using the COMP command to compare the files.

In versions 4.0+, DISKCOMP disregards differences in volume serial numbers.

See Also   COMP

DISKCOPY

Copies the contents of a floppy disk to another on a track-by-track basis.

● SYNTAX

DISKCOPY (*source drive:*) (*target drive:*) (/*options*)

If the source drive and the target drive parameters are the same, DOS first reads the floppy disk in the source drive, then prompts you to remove the disks and insert the target disk into the same drive. You may have to switch disks more than once to complete the copy process.

If you are logged onto a floppy-disk drive and invoke DISKCOPY without parameters, DOS prompts you to insert the source and target diskettes into the drive, as required. If you do not specify a target drive, DOS uses the currently logged floppy-disk drive for the target drive.

If the target disk is unformatted, DISKCOPY will format the disk first. To do so, FORMAT.COM or FORMAT.EXE must be available to DOS, either on the currently logged drive or the DOS search path.

● OPTIONS

/1   Instructs DISKCOPY to copy only the first side of each disk, even double-sided disks.

/V   Instructs DISKCOPY to perform a validity check on the data copied to the target disk. This extra step slows the copying process somewhat.

● EXAMPLES

DISKCOPY A:

copies the disk in drive A onto the disk in the currently logged drive. If the current drive is drive A, DISKCOPY prompts you to switch disks at various times during the copy process.

DISKCOPY A: B: /1

copies the disk in drive A onto the disk in drive B. Copies only the first side of the source disk.

● ERRORLEVEL CODES

0 = Copy completed successfully

1 = Read or write error caused differences between source and target

2 = Operator interrupted copy with Ctrl-C

3 = Copy interrupted by data errors or damaged disks

4 = Invalid drive letters, drive types, insufficient RAM, or syntax error

● ERROR MESSAGES

Cannot DISKCOPY to or from an ASSIGNed or SUBSTed drive

The source or target drive is assigned using the ASSIGN or SUBST command. Remove the assignments before re-invoking the DISKCOPY command.

Cannot DISKCOPY to or from a network drive

Do not attempt to invoke DISKCOPY on a drive that has been redirected over a network.

Diskette bad or incompatible

One of the disks has an incorrect format, is copy-protected, or contains data errors. If the disk is not copy-protected, use the CHKDSK command to attempt to correct the problems.

Do not specify filename(s)

Do not include file names with drive types when invoking the DISKCOPY command. Correct the syntax and try again.

Drive or diskette types not compatible

You have attempted to use the DISKCOPY command on drives with two different format types. Use the COPY or XCOPY command instead.

Specified drive does not exist, or is non-removable

You have invoked the DISKCOPY command using a fixed disk drive, or an invalid drive letter. DISKCOPY is intended for use on floppy disks only. Correct the syntax and try again.

Target disk may be unusable

DISKCOPY has detected data errors when copying the disk. The copy process is complete, but this message is a warning that the disk may not work properly. Format the disk and try again. This message can also appear when you attempt to copy a disk that is copy-protected.

● **USING THE DOS 5.0 SHELL**   You may copy disks within the DOS shell by selecting Disk Utilities from the Main program window, then selecting the Disk Copy Option. A dialog box appears, displaying the default parameters for the command. If you wish to enter new parameters, simply type them in. If you wish to edit the parameters, move the right or left arrow key before typing. When the parameters are correct, press Enter or select the OK box.

● **NOTES**   DISKCOPY will only copy floppy disks that are the same size and data density. For example, you cannot copy a 5.25", 360Kb floppy onto a 5.25", 1.2Mb floppy. You cannot copy hard disks or RAM disks using DISKCOPY.

You cannot use DISKCOPY on drives that have been reassigned using the ASSIGN, JOIN, or SUBST commands. You cannot use DISKCOPY to copy disks across a network.

You can copy the contents of one disk to another disk of a different size or density using the XCOPY or COPY commands. The target disk must be large enough to accommodate all the source files.

Disks made using DISKCOPY are track-and-sector duplicates of each other. This means that if there is a data error on the source disk, it most likely will be copied onto the target disk as well. Likewise, fragmented files on the source disk will be identically fragmented on the target disk.

If your version of DOS supports XCOPY, you can use that command instead, which will eliminate or call attention to some data errors and put together fragmented files on the target drive, with no significant loss of copying speed.

In versions 4.0+, DOS will create a new volume serial number on the target disk.

See Also   COPY, XCOPY

DOSKEY

| E |
| 5.0 |

Allows DOS to remember DOS commands, and permits the user to move the cursor along the command line, editing DOS commands before they are invoked.

• SYNTAX

DOSKEY (/*options*)

The DOSKEY command is normally invoked without options.

• USING DOSKEY Once invoked, DOSKEY saves previously invoked DOS commands in a special buffer in RAM. The user may recall these previous commands by scrolling through the buffer. Pressing the up arrow scrolls backward, pressing the down arrow scrolls forward.

Any command on the command line may be edited by moving the cursor to the appropriate point and retyping the correct characters. In DOSKEY's normal default state, typed characters will overstrike existing characters on the command line. If the user presses the Insert key, typed characters are inserted in place on the command line. Pressing Insert a second time returns to overstrike mode.

Each time the user enters a command, the command is added to DOSKEY's command buffer. This includes duplicate commands and edited commands.

DOSKEY uses about 4Kb of RAM. This amount can increase if you specify a large buffer size as a command line option.

DOSKEY does not affect the standard DOS function keys, but it adds two function keys of its own. Pressing F7 will display a list of all the DOS commands in the buffer, numbered by line. A small angle bracket (**>**) will appear after the number of the current command line. Pressing F9 will display the following prompt:

Line number:

If you know the line number of a particular command in the buffer, you may make that command current by entering its line number. The command line will be displayed after the DOS prompt, and you may invoke it by pressing Enter.

● OPTIONS

/INSERT	Changes command line editing to Insert mode as the default. Press the Insert key to toggle between Insert and Overstrike mode.
/OVERSTRIKE	Changes command line editing to Overstrike mode as the default. This is the default state if no options are used. Press the Insert key to toggle between Overstrike and Insert mode.
/REINSTALL	Installs an additional copy of DOSKEY in RAM. Clears the current command buffer. Resets new options if specified on the command line. Each time DOSKEY is reinstalled, it takes up an additional 4Kb of RAM, plus whatever size you specify for the buffer.
/BUFSIZE=*nnnn*	Specifies the size of the command buffer, where *nnnn* is the size in bytes. Default is 512 bytes. The buffer size may not be changed except when first installing or reinstalling DOSKEY.
/HISTORY	Displays all stored command lines.
/MACROS	Displays all Doskey macros.

● EXAMPLES

DOSKEY

installs the DOSKEY buffer in RAM.

DOSKEY /HISTORY

displays the contents of the command line buffer, without line numbers.

DOSKEY /REINSTALL /BUFSIZE=1024

installs an additional copy of DOSKEY, clears the command line buffer, and enlarges it to 1Kb.

● ERROR MESSAGES

DOSKEY stores invalid commands as well as valid ones. If you repeat an invalid DOS command using DOSKEY, it will display the error message associated with that command.

● USING THE DOS 5.0 SHELL   You may use DOSKEY within the DOS shell by selecting the DOS Command Prompt option from the Main Programs window, and then invoking the DOSKEY command from the DOS prompt. However, it is likely that you will find it more useful to load DOSKEY before entering the shell so that the full command line buffer will be available whenever you select the DOS Command Prompt option.

If you reinstall DOSKEY while in the secondary command processor, you will lose all the commands in the command line buffer, and unlike other DOS commands that affect the system environment, you will not regain the original DOSKEY buffer when you invoke EXIT to return to the shell. See the COMMAND entry for details regarding secondary command processors.

EXE2BIN

E

1.1+

Converts executable program files to binary-format BIN or COM files.

● SYNTAX

EXE2BIN (drive:\path\) source file (drive:\path\target file)

The EXE2BIN command requires the name of an executable program file; that is, a file with extension .EXE. It converts this file to a memory image of the program on disk. If you do not specify a target file, the target file will have the same name as the source file, with the extension .BIN. If the binary-format file conforms to the rules for loading by DOS, you can rename its extension to .COM, or specify a target file with this extension.

● EXAMPLES

EXE2BIN MY-PROG

converts MY-PROG.EXE to MY-PROG.BIN.

EXE2BIN MY-PROG MY-PROG.COM

converts MY-PROG.EXE to MY-PROG.COM.

● ERROR MESSAGES

File cannot be converted

The EXE file is not in the correct format for conversion using this command. Use a different EXE file.

Fixups needed - base segment hex:

You are converting a file that requires a load segment in RAM. Specify the absolute segment address where the COM file is to be loaded.

● USING THE DOS 5.0 SHELL   You may use EXE2BIN within the DOS shell by selecting the DOS Command Prompt option from the Main Programs window, and invoking the EXE2BIN command from the DOS prompt. To return to the shell, invoke the EXIT command.

• **NOTES** Binary-format files are subject to some rigid rules in order to be loaded by the DOS command processor: the EXE source file cannot be larger than 64Kb; it cannot contain a stack segment (an area of the program's allocated RAM used to store intermediate results of processing); no part of the program can relocate in RAM; the file should not contain any absolute RAM addresses (unless you have DOS version 4.0 or later and the capability of loading the binary-format file at a specific address in RAM); and if you intend for the binary-format file to be loaded by DOS, it must begin execution at hexadecimal position 100 in the file. Many executable files make use of a stack segment and use separate code and data segments, making them impossible to convert to binary-format files.

Binary-format files, because they are a representation of the program as it appears in RAM, are generally more efficient to load into RAM than executable files. They may also take up a little less space on disk.

This command is intended for programmers, especially those with assembly-language experience. Users who do not create programs are not likely to have need for it.

EXIT

Returns control from a secondary processor to the parent processor, if one exists. Otherwise, EXIT has no effect.

• **SYNTAX**

EXIT

EXIT accepts no parameters or options. It will return control of the computer to a parent processor only if a secondary processor has been previously enabled with the COMMAND command. When EXIT returns control to the parent processor, all variables and environment settings changed by the secondary processor are lost; settings return to those of the parent processor.

For details regarding secondary and parent processors, see the COMMAND entry.

● **USING THE DOS 5.0 SHELL**   EXIT is intended for use at the command prompt or from within batch files. It has no purpose while the DOS shell is displayed on the screen. If you selected the DOS Command prompt option from the Main Program window, you must enter EXIT at the DOS prompt to return to the shell.

● **NOTES**   It is not advisable to load terminate-and-stay-resident (TSR) software, such as DOSKEY or SIDEKICK, while a secondary processor is active. The changes in RAM may adversely affect the behavior of the parent processor. Some application programs allow you to access a DOS "shell" by loading a secondary processor while a portion of the application program remains active. Avoid loading TSR software under these circumstances.

See Also   COMMAND

FASTOPEN

E

3.3+

TSR

Enhances system performance by storing the hard disk locations of previously opened files and subdirectories in RAM, in order to speed up subsequent access of the same files and subdirectories.

● SYNTAX

FASTOPEN *drive*: (=(n1,n2) *drive*:=(n1,n2) *drive*:=(n1,n2) *drive*:=(n1,n2)) (/ *options*)

FASTOPEN requires, at a minimum, one hard-disk drive letter, for the drive whose file and subdirectory name locations will be stored in RAM. You may specify from 1 to 4 drives on the FASTOPEN command line. FASTOPEN will not work with floppy disks.

If you do not explicitly indicate the maximum number of stored file and directory name locations, the default on each drive is 48. You can change the number of stored locations by following the drive letter with an equal sign (=) and a number from 10 to 999 (shown as *n1* in the above syntax listing). However, if you are specifying more than one drive, the total of all stored locations cannot exceed 999.

If you are using DOS version 4.0 or later, you may indicate a second number (shown as *n2* in the above syntax listing) indicating the maximum number of buffers that will store the location of the fragmented parts of each file on each drive, in a range from 1 to 999. If you wish to indicate the number of these buffers to use, you must place both numbers within parentheses, and precede *n2* with a comma. As before, if you are specifying more than one hard drive, the total of *n2* for all drives cannot exceed 999.

You may specify either *n1* or *n2*, or both if desired.

● OPTIONS

/X (Versions 4.0+) Indicates that the file locations will be stored in expanded memory. You must have installed an expanded memory manager for this option to work, and the memory must conform to the LIM 4.0 expanded memory specification. Refer to the documentation of your expanded memory manager for details regarding the LIM 4.0 specification.

• EXAMPLES

FASTOPEN C:

sets up RAM to store the locations of the last 48 opened files on drive C.

FASTOPEN C:=150 D:=100 /X

sets up RAM to store the locations of the last 150 opened files on drive C, and the last 100 on drive D. RAM will use expanded memory to store the file locations.

FASTOPEN C:=(150,15)

sets up RAM to store the locations of the last 150 opened file and directory name locations and the last 15 file extent entries on the drive C.

FASTOPEN C:=(,15)

sets up RAM to store only the last 15 file extent entries for files on drive C.

• ERROR MESSAGES

Cannot use FASTOPEN for drive

You have specified a drive type other than a fixed, nonremovable type, or have attempted to use FASTOPEN with more than four of these drives, or have specified a drive that has been redirected over a network. Correct the command parameters and re-invoke the command.

FASTOPEN already installed

FASTOPEN is already resident in memory. There is no need to install it again.

Same drive specified more than once

You have attempted to invoke FASTOPEN for a previously specified drive. If you wish to change the options for the drive, first reboot the computer.

Too many drive entries

You have exceeded the maximum number of four allowed fixed drives. Do not attempt to initialize more than four.

Too many file/directory entries

You have exceeded the maximum number of 999 file or directory entries. Do not attempt to initialize more than this number.

● **USING THE DOS 5.0 SHELL**   You may use FASTOPEN within the DOS shell by selecting the DOS Command Prompt option from the Main Programs window, and invoking the FASTOPEN command from the DOS prompt. To return to the shell, invoke the EXIT command.

● **NOTES**   Each file name location will use 48 bytes of memory. If you indicate the maximum 999 files, you will use almost 48Kb of RAM. Each file extent entry will require another 16 bytes of RAM, or just under an additional 16Kb if you use the maximum of 999. In general, these high values, because of their costly RAM requirements, will reach a point of diminishing returns: they will not significantly enhance performance for the RAM they use, and may in some cases interfere with applications that have heavy RAM requirements of their own. Experiment to find the minimum numbers that will still enhance the performance of your system.

Do not use FASTOPEN with drives that have been reassigned using the ASSIGN, JOIN, or SUBST commands.

If you wish to change the FASTOPEN settings, you must reboot DOS first.

FC

E

4.0+

Matches the contents of two files, or sets of files, and reports the differences between them.

● SYNTAX

FC (/*options*) (*drive*:*path*\) *file(s)* (*drive**path*\) *file(s)*

FC requires the names of two files that you want to compare. You may include wildcard characters in the file names for comparison. If you do so, DOS compares the files that match each other within the naming convention represented by the wildcard characters.

If either file set is not on the current drive or subdirectory, you must explicitly name the drive or subdirectory location of the files.

Files with extensions .BIN, .COM, .EXE, .LIB, .OBJ, or .SYS are compared as binary files unless you explicitly instruct DOS, by means of option switches, to do otherwise. All other files are compared as ASCII files unless you explicitly instruct DOS to do a binary comparison.

● OPTIONS

/A   Condenses the report of differences when comparing ASCII files. Instructs DOS to display only the beginning and end of differing lines.

/B   Instructs DOS to perform a binary comparison: DOS compares the files byte-by-byte, and reports all differences between bytes at the same offset location in the two files. The /B switch cannot be used in combination with any other option switch, except the /*nnnn* switch.

/C   Instructs DOS to ignore case when comparing ASCII files. Characters in both files are treated as if they were uppercase.

/L   Forces an ASCII comparison of the files.

/LB *n*   Sets the maximum number of differing lines allowed in ASCII file comparisons. If differing lines exceed the number *n*, the comparison process ends. If this switch is not used, the default is 100 lines.

/N   Includes line numbers in an ASCII comparison report.

/T   Does not expand tabs to spaces in an ASCII comparison report. If this switch is not used, tabs are displayed as eight spaces.

/W   Condenses an ASCII comparison report by displaying all tabs and consecutive spaces as a single space. Tabs and spaces are only condensed in the display. Actual differences in spacing and tabulation in the files are recorded.

/*nnnn*   Indicates the number of lines (or bytes in binary format comparisons) that must match after a difference is recorded. If less than this number is found, the match is displayed in the report along with the differences. If this switch is not used, the default is 2.

● EXAMPLES

FC TEST.TXT TEST.BAK

performs an ASCII comparison between TEST.TXT and TEST.BAK.

FC /B TEST.TXT TEST.BAK

forces a binary comparison between TEST.TXT and TEST.BAK.

FC /C /L /N /W *.BIN *.BAK

forces an ASCII comparison between *.BIN and *.BAK, disregards character case, displays line numbers in the report, and condenses consecutive spaces.

● ERROR MESSAGES

Cannot open file - No such file or directory

DOS cannot find a file you specified. Check that the file location is correct, and that its name is spelled correctly.

(file) longer than (file)

The compared files are of two different sizes. The longer file's remaining data is not considered.

Incompatible switches

You have used mutually exclusive options on the command line. Review the syntax and enter the correct options.

Out of memory

FC has run out of available RAM; this can happen when comparing very long files. Obtain more memory before running FC on these files.

Resynch failed. Files are too different

There is not enough RAM to process the differences found between the specified files. Compare other files.

● USING THE DOS 5.0 SHELL   You may use FC within the DOS shell by selecting the DOS Command Prompt option from the Main Programs window, and invoking the FC command from the DOS prompt. To return to the shell, invoke the EXIT command.

● NOTES   Unlike the COMP command, FC will continue to report differences if more than 10 are found. FC can make comparisons of ASCII files on a line-by-line basis, and will compare files that are different sizes, ending the comparison when it reaches the end of the shorter file. The output report from FC can be quite long, and redirection to a disk file or the printer is advisable. Refer to the

sections titled "Piping" and "Redirecting Output" in Part 1 for details.

If you redirect the output report of an ASCII comparison to a disk file, avoid wildcard characters in the command line. You can easily exceed the available buffers, and some files matching the specification may not be compared.

See Also COMP

FIND

E

2.0+

Locates and displays all occurrences of a specified character string in a specified file.

● SYNTAX

FIND "*string*" (*drive:\ path \ file*) (/*options*)

FIND requires that you include a character string on the command line. The character string must be enclosed in quotation marks. It is case-sensitive, meaning that uppercase letters will not match lower-case letters. If the string contains quotation marks, they should be enclosed in another set of quotation marks.

If you include a file specification, DOS reads the file and reports all occurrences of the character string in the file. Wildcard characters are not allowed in the file name.

Alternatively, you may supply redirected output via piping from another command instead of a file, and FIND will report occurrences of the string in the output.

• OPTIONS

/C   Counts the number of lines in the file that contain a match for the character string, and reports the total only.

/I   (Version 5.0+) Ignores letter case when searching for matching strings.

/N   Includes line numbers in the report of matching strings. If you include this option with the /C option, it is ignored.

/V   Reports only those lines that do not contain a match for the specified string. If you include this option with the /C option, DOS counts the number of lines that do not contain a match and reports that total.

• EXAMPLES

FIND "FIND" SAMPLE.TXT /C

reports the total number of lines in SAMPLE.TXT that contain the string **FIND**.

FIND "Say""hello there"", DOS" SAMPLE.TXT

reports the lines in SAMPLE.TXT that contain the string **Say "hello there", DOS**. Notice that each double-quote character contained within the string is entered twice to include the additional quotation marks inside the test string.

CHKDSK /V ¦ FIND "BAK" /N

uses the output of the CHKDSK /V command and displays all lines that contain **BAK**. The display includes the relative line number of each line.

FIND "%%%%%" SAMPLE.TXT /C/V

reports the total number of lines in SAMPLE.TXT that do not contain the string **%%%%%**. Assuming that the string does not occur in the file, FIND therefore will report the number of lines in the file.

● **USING THE DOS 5.0 SHELL** You may use FIND within the DOS shell by selecting the DOS Command Prompt option from the Main Programs window, and then invoking the FIND command from the DOS prompt. To return to the shell, invoke the EXIT command.

FORMAT

⊙ Can overwrite or erase data!

Prepares a blank disk for receiving and storing data, or creates a new blank disk from a used one.

● **SYNTAX**

FORMAT *target drive*: (*/options*)

In DOS versions 3.0+, FORMAT requires that you specify a drive letter for the disk to format. If you are using an earlier version and do not specify a disk drive, FORMAT will format the disk in the default drive.

● **USING FORMAT**   When you run the FORMAT command to format your disks, FORMAT displays a message indicating the drive you are about to format, and prompts you to press Enter when ready to proceed. This gives you the opportunity to change the disk in the drive if necessary, or cancel the operation by pressing Ctrl-C.

When the formatting operation is complete, DOS displays a message showing the total number of bytes available on disk, how many bytes have been marked as "bad sectors" (that is, unusable because of some defect that DOS discovered), and how may bytes have been used by system files, if you indicated the /S option in the command line. In version 5.0, DOS also indicates how data may be allocated on the newly formatted disks. DOS then asks if you would like to format another disk using the same parameters. If you enter Y, you are prompted to insert another disk, press Enter, and the formatting process repeats. Otherwise, you are returned to the DOS prompt.

Always exercise extreme caution when using this command so that you do not accidentally format a disk that contains data you want to keep. DOS versions 4.0+ have an extra safety device regarding hard disks: if your hard disk has a volume label, DOS prompts you to enter the volume label before it proceeds with the format.

A separate utility command found in version 5.0, UNFORMAT, can help you recover from an accidental format in some cases.

Do not use the FORMAT command with drives that have been reassigned using the ASSIGN, JOIN, or SUBST commands.

● OPTIONS

/1   Formats a double-sided disk as a single-sided disk.

/4   Formats a single-density (160Kb) or double-density (360Kb) disk with the correct number of default tracks and sectors in a high-density (1.2Mb) drive.

/8   Formats 8 sectors per track on 5.25" floppy disks instead of the default, which is 9 for single- or double-density disks, or 15 for high-density disks. This option cannot be used with hard disks, nor can it be used with the /T or /V option.

/B   Formats a disk so as to leave room for the system files, although system files are not copied. Cannot be used with the /T or /S option. When you use this option, DOS formats the disk with the usual default number of sectors per track (9 or 15), but also adds instructions to utilize only 8 per track.

/F:*size*   (Versions 4.0+) Specifies the size, in kilobytes, of the disk to be formatted. Not to be used with /1, /8, /T, or /N options. The following parameters may be used for size:

> 160K = 5.25" single-sided, 8 sectors/track
>
> 180K = 5.25" single-sided, 9 sectors/track
>
> 320K = 5.25" double-sided, 8 sectors/track
>
> 360K = 5.25" double-sided, 9 sectors/track
>
> 720K = 3.5" double-sided, 9 sectors/track
>
> 1.2M = 5.25" high-density, 15 sectors/track
>
> 1.44M = 3.5" high-density, 15 sectors/track

/N:*nn*   Indicates the number of sectors per track, where *nn* is the number of sectors you specify. This option must be used together with the /T option. Do not use this parameter with the /8 or /B options.

/Q   Specifies that formatting does not reinitialize tracks
        and sectors on a previously formatted disk.

/S   Transfers DOS system files to the formatted disk.
        Intended to make the disk "bootable"—that is,
        capable of loading DOS into memory when the
        computer is booted up while the disk is in the
        default boot drive (usually drive A).

/T:*nn*   Indicates the number of tracks on the disk, where
        nn is the number of tracks that you specify. This
        option must be used together with the /N option.
        Do not use this parameter with the /8 or /B
        options.

/U   (Version 5.0+) Specifies unconditional reformatting.
        All data on a previously formatted disk is
        destroyed, and you will not be able to unformat
        this disk later.

/V   Prompts you to add a volume label to the disk after
        formatting. A volume label is a string, up to 11
        characters long, that can function as an identifying
        title for the disk. You cannot use the /V option
        with the /8 option.

/V:*label* (Versions 4.0+) Automatically adds a volume label
        to the disk after formatting, as indicated by :*label*.

● EXAMPLES

FORMAT A:

formats the disk in drive A, using current default parameters for
the drive type.

FORMAT A: /S /V

formats a disk in drive A, using current drive defaults, then copies
the system files to the disk, and prompts the user to enter a volume
label for that disk.

FORMAT A: /1 /8

formats a floppy disk in drive A as a single-sided disk with 8 sectors per track. This format may be required by some early PC systems.

FORMAT A: /4

FORMAT A: /F:360K

formats a 5.25" double-density (360Kb) disk in a high-density (1.2Mb) drive.

FORMAT A: /T:80 /N:9

FORMAT A: /F:720K

formats a 3.5" low-density (720Kb) disk in a high-density (1.44Mb) drive.

● ERRORLEVEL CODES

0 = Format successful

3 = Format interrupted by Ctrl-C

4 = Format interrupted by disk, data or other technical error

5 = User responded N to hard-disk safety prompt, "Proceed with format?"

● ERROR MESSAGES

Cannot FORMAT an ASSIGNed or SUBSTed drive

You have attempted to format a drive that was assigned using the ASSIGN or SUBST command. Remove the assignments before re-invoking FORMAT.

Disk unsuitable for system disk

The current disk has defects where the system files must reside. Use a different disk.

Error reading partition table

The hard disk's partition table is unusable. Use FDISK to set up the partition table before attempting to format the disk.

Invalid volume ID

You have attempted to format the fixed disk and entered an invalid volume ID string. Use the DIR or VOL command to determine the correct volume label, and try again.

Must enter both /T and /N parameters

If you include one of these parameters, you must include the other as well. Review the correct syntax and try again.

Track 0 bad - disk unusable

FORMAT has detected disk errors in a critical portion of the disk. Reboot the computer and try again. If the problem persists, discard the disk. If the problem occurs for an inordinate number of disks, have your floppy drive serviced.

Unable to write BOOT

FORMAT has detected disk errors in the DOS partition. Reboot the computer and try again. If the problem persists, discard the disk.

● **USING THE DOS 5.0 SHELL**   You may format disks within the DOS shell by selecting Disk Utilities from the Main Program window, then selecting the Format option. A dialog box appears, displaying the default parameter for the command, drive A. If you wish to enter new parameters, simply type them in. If you wish to edit the parameters, move the right or left arrow key before typing. When the parameters are correct, press Enter or select the OK box.

● **NOTES**   Technically speaking, the FORMAT command places a *high-level* format on the disk. This format divides the disk into a numbered grid of tracks and sectors that define separate physical locations for storing data. Before you can use FORMAT on hard disks, an underlying, or *low-level*, format must be completed. The low-level format is usually completed by the manufacturer or dealer before you purchase the disk. In some cases, for example, if a hardware malfunction has wiped out data on your hard disk, you may need to perform a low-level format before you can use FORMAT.

If you find that you cannot successfully format your hard-disk, or that you cannot get your computer to acknowledge the presence of a hard disk drive in your system, check with your hard disk's documentation or ask your dealer if a low-level format is required.

See Also   LABEL, UNFORMAT, VOLUME

GRAFTABL

E

3.0+

Loads an extended character set (ASCII codes greater than 127) that may be used by applications that require a color graphics adapter.

● SYNTAX

GRAFTABL (*code page*) (*/options*)

GRAFTABL may be called without parameters, whereupon it will load the extended character set into memory.

Alternatively, if your system supports more than one character set, you may specify the code page number of the character set you wish to load. Following are examples of valid code page numbers for international character sets:

437 = United States (This is the default if no code page is specified.)

850 = Multinational

860 = Portuguese

863 = Canadian/French

865 = Nordic

See the CHCP and NLSFUNC entries, as well as the COUNTRY command entry in Appendix B, for details regarding how to configure your system for international character sets.

• OPTIONS

/STATUS   Displays the number of the current extended character set, if one has been loaded.

• EXAMPLES

GRAFTABL

loads the current default extended character set.

GRAFTABL /STATUS

displays the currently loaded extended character set, or "none" if none are loaded.

• ERRORLEVEL CODES

0 = Character set successfully loaded

1 = Character set successfully loaded, replacing a previously-loaded character set

2 = Error occurred reading character set file

3 = Incorrect command line parameter; command aborted

4 = Incorrect DOS version

• USING THE DOS 5.0 SHELL   You may use GRAFTABL within the DOS shell by selecting the DOS Command Prompt option from the Main Programs window, and invoking the GRAFTABL command from the DOS prompt. However, because GRAFTABL changes the operating system environment, which is used under these circumstances by a secondary command processor, its settings will remain in effect only until you return to the shell using the EXIT command.

Upon return to the shell, the information loaded in memory by GRAFTABL will be discarded, along with the secondary command processor. See the COMMAND entry for details regarding secondary command processors.

GRAPHICS

E

2.0+

Allows graphics characters to be sent to an IBM-compatible graphics printer using Shift-Prtsc.

● SYNTAX

GRAPHICS (*printer*) (/*options*)

Used without parameters, the GRAPHICS command will allow the Shift-Prtsc key combination to send screen graphics characters to an IBM graphics printer, or a printer that is fully compatible. In addition, to use this command, you must have a monitor that can display the IBM graphics character set.

You may specify the following alternate types of IBM graphics printers on the command line:

COLOR1 = IBM color printer with black ribbon

COLOR4 = IBM color printer with red, green, blue, black ribbon

COLOR8 = IBM color printer with cyan, magenta, yellow, black ribbon

COMPACT = IBM Compact Printer

GRAPHICS = IBM Standard Graphics Printer, or Proprinter

THERMAL = IBM Convertible Printer

Version 5.0 allows for many other printer types. Refer to the DOS documentation to see if your printer type is listed.

● OPTIONS

/R   Reverses foreground and background. Normally, the screen shows light characters on a dark background. When printing, the light characters print as dark characters and the background is not printed. If you would like the printed output to resemble the appearance of the screen more closely, use this switch to print light characters on a dark background.

/B   Prints background color. This option is only available with the COLOR4 and COLOR8 printers. If you do not specify this switch, the background is not printed.

/LCD   Prints characters from the IBM PC Convertible Liquid Crystal Display.

/PRINTBOX:*nn*   (Versions 4.0+) Selects the size of the print box, where *nn* is the printbox I.D. number, the first parameter following the Printbox Statement in your printer profile. Refer to your printer's configuration documentation for details regarding the Printbox Statement. If you are using DOS 5.0's GRAPHICS.PRO file for your printer information, *nn* is either STD or LCD.

● EXAMPLES

GRAPHICS

allows Shift-Prtsc to send IBM graphics characters to an IBM Graphics Printer.

GRAPHICS COLOR4 /B

prints on the red, green, blue, black IBM color printer, including background color.

GRAPHICS THERMAL /LCD

prints on the IBM Convertible thermal printer from the IBM convertible liquid crystal display.

● ERROR MESSAGES

/B invalid with black and white printer

You cannot specify a background color on a black-and-white printer. Re-invoke the command without the /B option.

Error reading GRAPHICS profile

DOS cannot find the printer profile file for use with the GRAPHICS command. Be certain the printer profile file and GRAPHICS.COM are on the same subdirectory.

Invalid profile statement on line x

There is an incorrect syntax in the graphics profile file, where x is the location of the incorrect line. Edit the file and try again. If editing with a word processor, be sure that you save the file in ASCII format.

Printbox ID not in GRAPHICS profile

The printbox ID number is not correct. Check the ID number in the printer profile; correct the syntax and try again.

Unable to reload with profile specified

You have attempted to load a different graphics profile without allowing sufficient memory. Reboot the computer and try again.

● USING THE DOS 5.0 SHELL   You may use GRAPHICS
within the DOS shell by selecting the DOS Command Prompt option

from the Main Programs window, and then invoking the GRAPH-ICS command from the DOS prompt. However, because GRAPHICS changes the operating system environment, which is used under these circumstances by a secondary command processor, it will affect only those screen dumps that you initiate before returning to the shell. When you return to the shell using the EXIT command, the information loaded in memory by GRAPHICS will be discarded along with the secondary command processor. See the COMMAND entry for details regarding secondary command processors.

● **NOTES**   GRAPHICS increases the size of DOS in RAM by about 700 bytes.

GRAPHICS requires that your computer have a graphics adapter and monitor. Versions 4.0+ support EGA and VGA graphics modes.

See Also   GRAFTABL

HELP

I
5.0

Displays short summaries of command syntax.

● **SYNTAX**

HELP (*command*)

Invoke the HELP command without parameters to list all the standard DOS line and batch commands. To receive help with a particular command, enter HELP followed by the command name. Alternatively, you may enter the command name, followed by /?.

● EXAMPLES

HELP > PRN

lists standard DOS commands, with a brief description of each, and directs the output to the default printing device.

HELP DOSKEY

displays a short description of DOSKEY command syntax.

DOSKEY /?

is an alternate means of displaying a short description of DOSKEY command syntax.

● **NOTES** The online HELP command does not support CONFIG.SYS commands, ANSI.SYS escape sequences, or installable device driver syntax.

JOIN

```
E
```
```
2.0+
```

Substitutes a subdirectory name for a drive letter.

• SYNTAX

JOIN (*source drive:*) (*target drive:\ subdirectory*) (/ *options*)

The JOIN command is used to enable programs written only for floppy disks to operate on a hard-disk system by substituting a subdirectory name in place of the floppy-drive letter. After you invoke JOIN, subsequent calls to the specified drive will go to the subdirectory instead.

To substitute a subdirectory name for a drive letter, invoke JOIN, followed by the drive letter, followed by the name of a subdirectory path. The subdirectory path parameter should include a drive letter and name of an existing subdirectory. The subdirectory you specify must be empty, and must be nested just below the root directory. The root directory itself, as well as all other nesting levels of subdirectories, are not allowed. If you invoke the JOIN command without parameters, DOS displays the names of any drives that are currently joined to subdirectories.

• OPTIONS

/D   Cancels the effects of the JOIN command. Use this option with the drive letter you intend to disconnect from a subdirectory.

• EXAMPLES

JOIN A: C:\ A_DRIVE

joins drive A to the A_DRIVE subdirectory on hard-disk C. All further calls to drive A will reference C:\A_DRIVE instead.

JOIN A: /D

disconnects the effect of the previous example.

• ERROR MESSAGES

Cannot JOIN a network drive

You cannot use the JOIN command on drives that have been redirected over a network.

Directory not empty

You have attempted to JOIN a directory containing files (possibly hidden files; use DIR /A:H to reveal them). Select or create an empty directory and try again.

• USING THE DOS 5.0 SHELL   You may use JOIN within the DOS shell by selecting the DOS Command Prompt option from the Main Programs window, and then invoking the JOIN command from the DOS prompt. However, because JOIN changes the operating system environment, it will affect only those applications that you execute before returning to the shell. When you return to the shell using the EXIT command, the information loaded in memory by JOIN will be discarded, along with the secondary command processor. See the COMMAND entry for details regarding secondary command processors.

• NOTES   The following DOS commands will not work when floppy drives have been redirected to subdirectories with the JOIN command: BACKUP, CHKDSK, DISKCOMP, DISKCOPY, FDISK, FORMAT, LABEL, RECOVER, RESTORE, and SYS.

The SUBST and ASSIGN commands will work with JOIN, but can create unnecessary confusion by sending files to unwanted locations. Use JOIN only when you absolutely must, and exercise extreme caution.

KEYB

E
3.3+
TSR

Loads a nonstandard keyboard configuration into memory. The loaded configuration is taken from a library file, usually KEYBOARD.SYS.

● SYNTAX

KEYB (*keyboard*) (*,code page*) (*drive*:\ *path*\ *library file*) (/*ID*:*nnn*)(/E)

When invoked without parameters, KEYB displays the name of the currently logged nonstandard keyboard, if one is loaded.

The *keyboard* parameter is a two-letter code indicating the nonstandard keyboard you want to load. If loading from KEYBOARD.SYS (the default keyboard library file), this code will represent a country, as shown in Table 2.1.

The *code page* parameter is required in DOS version 3.3, and is optional thereafter. It is a three-digit number representing a table that defines a foreign language character set to be used by the keyboard. The code page numbers were revised after they were introduced in version 3.3. Refer to Table 2.1 for the correct code pages for versions 3.3+.

The *library file* parameter is only used if the library file is not KEYBOARD.SYS, or if the location of the library file is not on the operating system's search path. See the PATH entry for more information regarding search paths.

Table 2.1: Nonstandard Keyboard Codes in DOS 3.3+

COUNTRY CODE	KEYBOARD	CODE PAGE (3.3 / 4.0+)	ID # (4.0+)
United States (default)	US	001 / 437	103
Belgium	BE	032 / 437	120
Canadian (French)	CF	002 / 863	058
Denmark	DK	045 / 865	159
Finland	SU	358 / 437	153
France	FR	033 / 437	189
Germany	GR	049 / 437	129
Italy	IT	039 / 437	141
Latin America	LA	003 / 437	171
Netherlands	NL	031 / 437	143
Norway	NO	047 / 865	155
Portugal	PO	351 / 860	163
Spain	SP	034 / 437	172
Sweden	SV	046 / 437	153
Swiss (French)	SF	041 / 437	150
Swiss (German)	SG	041 / 437	000
United Kingdom	UK	044 / 437	166

● OPTIONS

/E   Specifies that an enhanced keyboard is installed
            on an Intel 8086-based (XT-type) computer.

/ID:*nnn*   (Versions 4.0+) Use the ID switch to designate the currently logged keyboard by means of its three-digit ID number (which is not the same as the code page), where *nnn* is the chosen ID number. This switch is used in addition to the standard two-letter keyboard code.

● EXAMPLES

KEYB

displays the currently installed nonstandard keyboard configuration, if any.

KEYB UK,044

installs the United Kingdom keyboard in version 3.3.

KEYB UK

installs the United Kingdom keyboard in versions 4.0 and later.

KEYB UK,437 /ID:166

is an optional syntax that will install the United Kingdom keyboard in versions 4.0 and later.

● ERRORLEVEL CODES

0 = Installation was successful

1 = Invalid command line syntax

2 = Keyboard library file not found or invalid

3 = Could not load keyboard configuration

4 = Error with console device

5 = Requested code page not prepared

6 = Code Page table not found

7 = Incorrect DOS version

● ERROR MESSAGES

Bad or missing keyboard definition file

KEYB could not find the KEYBOARD.SYS file, or it has become corrupted. Be sure that KEYBOARD.SYS is located in the same sub-directory as KEYB.EXE. If it's necessary, copy a new KEY-BOARD.SYS file from backup.

Code page is not valid

The current code page is not compatible with the requested key-board code page. Change the code page parameter and try again.

Code page has not been designated or prepared

KEYB does not recognize a parameter that you entered. If neces-sary, prepare the code page for your display device using the MODE CODEPAGE PREPARE command, then re-invoke the KEYB command using the correct code page parameter.

Code page is not consistent

The current code page is not compatible with the requested key-board code page. Change the code page parameter and try again; if necessary, prepare the correct code page using MODE CODEPAGE PREPARE.

One or more CON code pages invalid

This is a warning that some prepared code pages will not work with the current KEYB code page. Be certain that you change the keyboard code page to those prepared code pages that are compatible.

Unable to create KEYB table in resident memory

There is not enough memory to make room for the requested key-board code page. Check the amount of memory. If necessary, clear out other memory-resident applications, or reboot the computer to make room.

● USING THE DOS 5.0 SHELL   The standard DOS shell has
no provision for loading nonstandard keyboards, but you may add commands to do so. See Part 3, "The DOS Shell," for details on ad-ding commands.

● **NOTES**   Once a nonstandard keyboard is loaded, you can switch between the standard and nonstandard keyboard configurations. Press Ctrl-Alt-F1 to switch to the standard keyboard; press Ctrl-Alt-F2 to switch to the nonstandard configuration. DOS will not display any messages when you switch.

In DOS 3.0, the two-character keyboard code was included in the DOS command. The following nonstandard keyboards were supported:

Keyboard	Version 3.0 Command
France	KEYBFR
Germany	KEYBGR
Italy	KEYBIT
Spain	KEYBSP
United Kingdom	KEYBUK

LABEL

E

3.0+

Adds or modifies a disk volume label.

● **SYNTAX**

LABEL *target drive*: (*label*)

The LABEL command requires a drive letter on the command line. If you include the optional *label* parameter, DOS writes the specified volume label on the disk indicated by the drive letter. If you do not include the *label* parameter on the command line, DOS prompts you to enter the volume label. If you press Enter without entering a volume label, DOS assumes that you want to delete the current label, and prompts you to confirm the deletion. If you want to delete the current label, enter Y. Otherwise, enter N.

A disk volume label may be up to 11 characters long, and may include spaces. Do not use tabs or the following punctuation marks in a volume label:

   * ? & ^ / \ | , . ; : < > [ ] ( ) + = "

The space character and the following punctuation marks *are* valid:

   ! _ @ # $ % ~ ' - { }

● EXAMPLES

LABEL C:

will cause DOS to prompt you to enter a volume label for a disk in drive C (often a hard disk).

LABEL C:MY DATA

will write the volume label "MY DATA" on the disk in drive C.

● ERROR MESSAGES

Cannot LABEL a network drive

You cannot use the LABEL command on drives that have been redirected over a network.

Cannot LABEL an ASSIGNed or SUBSTed drive

You have attempted to add or edit a label on a drive that was assigned using the ASSIGN or SUBST command. Remove the assignments before re-invoking LABEL.

Invalid characters in volume label

The LABEL command cannot accept some of the characters you have entered, or you have exceeded the limit of eleven characters. Check the list of valid characters and try again.

● **USING THE DOS 5.0 SHELL**   The standard DOS shell has
no provision for writing volume labels, but you may add commands
to do so. See Part 3, "The DOS Shell," for details on adding commands.

● **NOTES**   Do not use LABEL on drives that have been reassigned using the JOIN or SUBST commands.

See Also   DIR, VOL

LH OR LOADHIGH

I

5.0

TSR

Loads terminate-and-stay-resident (TSR) software into reserved
memory.

● **SYNTAX**

LH (*drive*:\ *path*\) *program*
LOADHIGH (*drive*:\ *path*\) *program*

TSR software is normally loaded into *conventional memory*, which is
the area of RAM from 0 to 640Kb. The LH and LOADHIGH commands attempt to load the TSR program specified in the *program*
parameter into *reserved memory*, the area of RAM between 640Kb
and 1024Kb, provided that DOS can find available space. Otherwise, the program is loaded in conventional memory.

To use this command, you must first have loaded the HIMEM.SYS device driver plus an expanded memory manager that supports the Microsoft Extended Memory Specification for upper memory blocks; for example, EMM386.EXE, which is supplied with MS-DOS. Use CONFIG.SYS to load these driver files. In addition, you must also include the UMB parameter in the DOS= command line in CONFIG.SYS. Refer to Appendix B for details on the DEVICE= and DOS= commands in CONFIG.SYS, and Appendix C for details regarding HIMEM.SYS and EMM386.EXE.

● EXAMPLES

LH MOUSE

loads the mouse driver software into reserved memory.

● **NOTES** Not all TSR software can be loaded in reserved memory. To see if your software can utilize reserved memory, try the following: reboot, load the program with LOADHIGH, and invoke the MEM command. Note the amount of available conventional memory. Then reboot again, load the program normally, and invoke MEM. If MEM reports a greater amount of conventional RAM after loading with LOADHIGH than it does after loading the program normally, then LOADHIGH is loading the program in reserved memory.

See Also DEVICEHIGH (Appendix B)

LOADFIX

Runs application software that may not load properly when DOS 5.0 occupies high memory.

● SYNTAX

LOADFIX (*drive:\path***) program**

LOADFIX causes external applications to be loaded above the first 64Kb of conventional memory. Most applications have no need for LOADFIX.

If you try to run a program that ran under an earlier version of DOS and receive a "Packed file corrupt" message under DOS 5.0, try invoking the program with LOADFIX.

● EXAMPLES

LOADFIX FASTBACK

loads FASTBACK.EXE in conventional memory.

● USING DOS 5.0 SHELL   You may use LOADFIX within the DOS shell by selecting the DOS Command Prompt option from the Main Programs window and invoking the LOADFIX command from the DOS prompt. Refer to Part 3 for instructions on adding commands to a shell program group.

MD OR MKDIR

I
2.0+

Creates a new subdirectory.

● SYNTAX

MD (*drive*:\ *path*) *new directory name*
MKDIR (*drive*:\ *path*) *new subdirectory name*

MD requires that you provide a subdirectory name on the command line. If the subdirectory name is preceded by a backslash (\), it will be created one level below the root directory. If the name is preceded by a space, it will be created one level below the currently logged subdirectory.

If you include an existing subdirectory path, the new subdirectory will be created one level below the indicated path. If you include a drive letter, the subdirectory will be created on the existing drive.

● EXAMPLES

MD TEXT

creates a subdirectory named TEXT one level below the currently logged subdirectory.

MD \TEXT

creates a subdirectory named TEXT one level below the root directory.

MD \DATA\TEXT

creates a subdirectory named TEXT one level below the DATA sub-directory, if the DATA subdirectory already exists.

MD C:\DATA\TEXT

creates a subdirectory named TEXT one level below the DATA sub-directory on drive C, if C:\DATA already exists.

● ERROR MESSAGES

Unable to create directory

MD has either found a directory with the same name and path loca-tion, or the disk might be full. To correct the first problem, use a dif-ferent directory name; to correct the latter, use a different disk or erase some files.

● USING THE DOS 5.0 SHELL   Select the Directory Tree win-
dow. Highlight the parent directory by pointing to it and clicking the mouse once or press the up or down arrow key until the directory is highlighted. Select File from the menu bar, then select Create

Directory. When the dialog box appears, enter the name of the directory you want to create. Press Enter, or select the OK box. To cancel the command, select the Cancel box.

See Also   CD or CHDIR

MEM

4.0+

Displays information on allocation of random access memory.

● SYNTAX

MEM (/*options*)

When invoked without option switches, MEM displays a summary of the amount and type of installed memory.

● OPTIONS

/C	Use this switch to list currently loaded programs, including the amount of memory each is using.
/CLASSIFY	Same as the /C option.
/program	Lists currently loaded programs, including their RAM addresses. /P also specifies this command.
/debug	Lists programs and system device drivers, including their RAM addresses. /D also specifies this command.

You cannot use both /program and /debug switches on the same command line.

● EXAMPLES

MEM /PROGRAM

lists the amount and type of installed RAM, and how it is allocated among loaded programs.

● USING THE DOS 5.0 SHELL

The standard DOS shell has no provision for displaying RAM allocations, but you may add this command to the shell if you so desire. See Part 3, "The DOS Shell," for details.

● NOTES

MEM finds extended memory above 1Mb if installed. MEM will only find expanded memory that conforms to the LIM 4.0 expanded memory specification. Refer to your expanded memory driver documentation for details.

MIRROR

E
5.0
TSR

Stores root directory and file allocation tables (FAT) in a safe area of the disk, to be used to recover in case of an accidental reformat (see UNFORMAT).

● SYNTAX

MIRROR (*drive:*) (/*options*)

If invoked without parameters, MIRROR stores the root directory and FAT for the currently logged drive. If you specify a drive letter, the information on that drive is stored. If you re-invoke MIRROR, the drive information is recorded in a new file, and the previous information is saved in a file with a .BAK extension.

● OPTIONS

/1	Saves only the current file; deletes BAK file.
/T*drive-nnn*	Installs resident tracking module for automatic updating of a drive's root directory and FAT, where *drive:* is the drive to track, and *nnn* is the maximum number of files to be tracked.
/U	Unloads resident tracking module, if possible.
/PARTN	Saves the hard-disk partition tables onto a floppy disk.

● EXAMPLES

MIRROR

records the directory and FAT information for the currently logged drive.

MIRROR /TC-999

records the directory and FAT information for drive C, and tracks changes to the information for up to 999 files on the drive.

● USING THE DOS 5.0 SHELL   Within the DOS shell, you
may invoke MIRROR from the DOS prompt after pressing Shift-F9. However, do not initialize the resident tracking and update features from the shell, as this may lead to memory conflicts. If you want to use the automatic tracking features, invoke the command before you enter the shell.

See Also UNFORMAT

MODE

E

1.0+

TSR

Performs various functions relating to the transfer of data between the processor and the screen, and the printer and keyboard. Specifically, the MODE command

- Sets the parallel printer mode
- Sets serial communication protocols
- Redirects parallel printer output
- Sets the video mode
- Shifts screen left or right
- Sets screen length and width
- Prepares and selects code pages
- Sets key repetition rates
- Displays the status of attached devices

● SYNTAX

To set the parallel printer mode (versions 3.3 and earlier):

MODE lpt*n*(:) (*characters per line*) (*,lines per inch*) (*,P*)

You must indicate the parallel printer device name, where *n* is a number from 1 to 3; for example, LPT1. The colon following the number is optional. The remaining parameters may be included if your printer can accept the indicated values. The *characters per line* parameter may be 80 or 132. The *lines per inch* parameter may be 6 or 8. You may specify the *P* parameter to indicate that DOS should repeat its instruction to send data indefinitely, in the event that the printer is not ready to receive the data for any reason.

To set the parallel printer mode (versions 4.0 and later):

MODE lpt*n*(:) (cols=*n*) (lines=*n*) (retry=*x*)

As in the previous syntax for this command, you must specify a parallel printer device name as LPT followed by a number from 1 to 3, depending on the number of parallel ports on your system. The *n* in Cols=*n* indicates the number of columns (always equal to the number of text characters) per line. The *n* in Lines=*n* indicates the number of printed lines per inch. Retry=*x* indicates how DOS should react if the printer is not accepting data, where *x* is replaced with one of four possible parameters:

B	Retries sending data if the printer is busy until printer accepts it.
E	Returns a DOS error message indicating that the printer is not accepting data.
R	Resets the port to "Ready" status; sends the data.
(no letter)	Indicates that DOS should not retry sending data. This aborts data transmission to the printer port with the "Abort, Retry, Ignore, Fail?" error message.

To set serial communication protocols (versions 3.3 and earlier):

MODE com*n*(:) *baud rate* (*,parity*) (*,data bits*) (*,stop bits*) (*,P*)

Before you initialize serial communication settings, refer to your documentation for the peripheral device to determine the correct setting for these parameters. The parameters after the COM port parameter are supplied in the order shown above, separated by commas.

The first parameter indicates the communication port that you want to use, where *n* after COM is the number of the port. You must also specify the applicable baud rate. You may provide the other command line parameters explicitly, separated by commas, or you may supply only the commas, which will cause DOS to accept default values. You may set one of three types of *parity*, depending on what is required by the peripheral (the default is even parity):

N   No parity

O   Odd parity

E   Even parity

You may set either 7 or 8 *databits* (the default is 7). If you want to send binary data (for example, downloading font files to a laser printer), use 8. You may set 1 or 2 *stopbits*. (The default is 2 when the baud rate is 110; otherwise, the default is 1.) If you are setting these parameters for a printer, supply the ,P parameter so that DOS will continue to retry sending the data until the printer accepts it.

To set serial communication protocols (versions 4.0 and later):

MODE com*n*(:) (baud=*nnnn*) (data=*n*) (stop=*n*) (parity=*x*) (retry=*x*)

The *n* in com*n* is the number of the COM port. Baud=*nnnn* indicates the baud rate. Data=*n* indicates the number of databits, where *n* is a value from 5 through 8 (the default is 7). Stop=*n* indicates the number of stopbits, where *n* is either 1, 1.5, or 2. (The default is 2 if the baud rate is 110; otherwise, it is 1.) Parity=*x* indicates the parity type, where *x* can be one of the following values:

NONE   No parity

ODD   Odd parity

EVEN   Even parity

MARK   Stick Odd parity

SPACE   Stick Even parity

Retry=*x* is used if the peripheral device is a printer. It indicates how DOS should react if the printer is not accepting data, where *x* is replaced with one of four possible parameters, the same as those used with the retry=*x* argument when setting parallel communication protocols in versions 4.0 and later.

To redirect parallel printer output to a serial port (all versions):

MODE lpt*n*(:)=com*n*(:)

You must specify a valid parallel and serial port number for your system, where *n* is the port number. Before directing parallel output to a serial port, use the MODE command to initialize the serial communications parameters, as explained earlier.

To set the video mode (all versions):

MODE *video mode* (,*length*) (,*shift*) (,T)

MODE does not support all types of video monitors, particularly the newer EGA, VGA, and XGA types. The *video mode* parameter may be one of several possible values. For example, 40 equals the standard 40-column display, and 80 equals the standard 80-column display. Refer to your DOS manual for other values.

The optional *length* parameter indicates the number of lines that your monitor can display. It may be supplied only if the ANSI.SYS device driver was loaded in the CONFIG.SYS file. See Appendix B, "CONFIG.SYS Commands," and Appendix C, "Standard MS-DOS Device Driver Files," for details. The screen length may be any number of lines that your monitor is capable of displaying; refer to your monitor and graphics card documentation for details.

The optional *shift* parameter shifts the screen display one or two characters to the right or left. Replace *shift* with R to shift right or L to shift left. This parameter cannot be used on the same command line with the *length* parameter; use one or the other, not both. If you use the *shift* parameter, you may also supply the optional *T* parameter. If this parameter is supplied, MODE will display a test pattern on the screen, allowing you to visualize the results of the shifting.

To set screen length and width (versions 4.0 and later):

MODE CON (lines=*nn*) (cols=*nn*)

This command will work only if the ANSI.SYS device driver was loaded in the CONFIG.SYS file. You must use CON as the first parameter to indicate that you are setting lines and columns for the console device. The *nn* in Lines=*nn* indicates the number of screen lines to display. (Be certain that your monitor is capable of displaying the number of lines you specify.) The *nn* in Cols=*nn* indicates the number of screen columns, or number of characters per line, to display.

To prepare code pages (foreign character sets) for use by a peripheral device (versions 3.3 and later):

MODE *device* **CODEPAGE PREPARE=((***code page list***)**
(*drive***: \ ***path***) \ ***file***)**

The *device* parameter indicates one of the standard DOS output devices (CON, PRN, or LPT1–3). Serial communications ports are not a valid device in this context.

A *code page* is a three-digit number referencing a particular foreign character set used by the printer, screen, or keyboard. Table 2.1 (see the KEYB entry) includes code pages for various foreign fonts in DOS versions 3.3 and later. Refer to the CHCP, KEYB, and NLSFUNC commands, as well as the COUNTRY command in Appendix B, for more details on foreign fonts and how they are used. The *code page list* parameter consists of any number of valid code pages, separated by commas.

Following the code page list, include the name of the code page information file. This file has a .CPI extension, and contains the device definitions attached to the foreign fonts you have specified. The CPI extension is not required, but you must include a drive letter and subdirectory path if the code page information file is not located on the currently logged drive and path.

To make a particular code page active in all versions:

MODE *device* **CODEPAGE SELECT=***nnn*

The *device* parameter indicates one of the standard DOS output devices (CON, PRN, LPT1–3) for which a code page has been previously prepared, where *nnn* indicates the number of the prepared code page to make active. You may substitute CP for CODEPAGE and SEL for SELECT in the above syntax.

To reinstate a code page that has been lost in all versions:

MODE *device* **CP REFRESH**

To see a display of the current code page setup (versions 4.0 and later):

MODE *device* /STATUS

The *device* parameter indicates one of the standard DOS output devices (CON, PRN, LPT1–3) for which a code page has been prepared.

To set key repetition rates (versions 4.0 and later):

MODE CON RATE=*nn* DELAY=*n*

where *nn* indicates the approximate number of times per second (1 to 32) a key will repeat when it is held down. The number supplied in place of *nn* does not correspond to the actual number of times per second the key repeats. Refer to your DOS manual for a comparison of these numbers and actual key repetition rates. DELAY=*n* indicates the amount of time required to hold a key down before it begins repeating, where *n* is a delay value. The range of valid delay values is from 1 to 4, where 1 equals ¼ second, 2 equals $1/2$ second, 3 equals ¾ second, and 4 equals 1 second.

To display the status of a particular device on all versions:

MODE (*device*) (/STATUS)

The *device* parameter indicates the device whose status you want to check. Valid device names are CON, PRN, LPT1–3, and COM1–4. The /STATUS parameter is used only when the output of the device you are checking was previously redirected to another device.

• EXAMPLES

MODE COM1 9600,N,8,1,P

sets the communication protocol on the first serial port to 9600 baud, no parity, eight databits, and one stop bit, for a printing device (versions 3.3 and earlier).

MODE COM1 BAUD=9600 DATA=8 STOP=1 PARITY=NONE RETRY=B

does the same thing in versions 4.0 and later.

MODE LPT1=COM1

redirects standard parallel printer output to the first serial port.

MODE CON CODEPAGE PREP=((865,437) C:\DOS\EGA)

prepares the code pages for Denmark and Germany for use by an EGA-type display device in DOS version 4.0 and later. (The code page file is named EGA.CPI, located on the C:\DOS subdirectory.)

MODE CON RATE=25 DELAY=1

sets keyboard repetition rates to 16 per second after holding the key down for 1/4 second (versions 4.0 and later).

MODE CON

checks the status of the console.

MODE LPT1 /STATUS

checks the status of the parallel printer after its output is redirected to a serial port.

● ERROR MESSAGES

Baud rate required

Specify a baud rate when using MODE to initialize a COM port.

Code pages cannot be prepared

You have entered duplicate code pages, invalid code pages, or too many code pages. Use the /STATUS option to find out which code pages have been prepared. Check the COUNTRY.SYS command line in the CONFIG.SYS file to determine how many code pages are allowed. Correct the syntax and try again.

Device error

The specified device may not support code page switching, or may have been incorrectly defined in CONFIG.SYS. Check the installation syntax for the device in CONFIG.SYS, correct it if necessary, and re-invoke the command.

Device or code page missing

DOS could not find the requested code page definition. Correct the code page parameter and re-invoke the MODE command for all desired code pages.

Device not prepared

You have attempted to use MODE SELECT for a code page that has not been prepared. Correct the code page parameter if necessary, or prepare the desired code page using MODE PREPARE.

Font file invalid

DOS cannot find the requested font file, or the font file has become corrupted. Make sure the font file is on the same subdirectory as the MODE command. If necessary, copy a new font file from backup. Prepare once more all code pages with MODE PREPARE.

LPT not rerouted

MODE failed to redirect the parallel printer output. Check that your command parameters are all correct, and try again.

Requested screen shift out of range

You cannot shift the screen right or left any further. Correct the syntax and try again.

● **USING THE DOS 5.0 SHELL**   The standard DOS shell has no provision for using the MODE command, although some display changes are offered. You may add specific MODE commands to the DOS shell if you like. See Part 3, "The DOS Shell," for details on adding commands.

MORE

E

2.0+

Forces DOS to display output one screen at a time instead of continuous scrolling.

• SYNTAX

MORE < (*drive***:\ ***path***\ )***file(s)*

Alternate syntax:

command (parameter(s)) ¦ **MORE**

There are two ways to use the MORE command:

- If you would like to display the contents of a data file on the screen, enter MORE followed by the redirection symbol for input (<), then by the name of the file. Wildcard characters are not allowed.

- If you would like to display the output of another command, enter the command and any required parameters followed by the redirection symbol for piping (¦), then by MORE.

When you use MORE to display output, the display will stop each time the screen fills with information. To continue the display, press any key.

• EXAMPLES

MORE < REPORT.TXT

displays the contents of REPORT.TXT on the screen, pausing each time the screen is full.

TYPE REPORT.TXT ¦ MORE

has the same result as the previous example. In this case, the output of the TYPE command is redirected to MORE.

DIR ¦ MORE

displays the current file directory, pausing each time the screen is full.

● **USING THE DOS 5.0 SHELL** To view the contents of a file in the DOS shell, highlight the selected file in the File Directory window, then press the F9 function key. Alternatively, you can highlight the file, select File from the menu bar, then select View file contents from the File pull-down menu. To scroll through the file press the PgUp or PgDn keys as required. When you finish viewing the file, press Esc, or select View from the menu bar, then select Restore view.

If you intend to redirect the output of other commands to MORE, you will need to add the specific command sequence to the disk utilities window. See Part 3, "The DOS Shell," for details on changing the display and adding commands.

See Also   TYPE

MSHERC

| E |

| 5.0 |

| TSR |

Installs functions for use with programs that require the Hercules Graphics Card.

● **SYNTAX**

MSHERC (/half)

Invoking MSHERC installs Hercules Graphics Card functions to assist DOS with running programs that use them. If you are using a 2-monitor system, include the /half parameter.

• USING THE DOS 5.0 SHELL   Invoke MSHERC before entering the DOS shell, to prevent memory conflicts after the shell is loaded.

NLSFUNC

E

3.3+

TSR

Loads national language support functions, allowing you to switch international character set tables in RAM.

• SYNTAX

NLSFUNC (*drive:\path\country file***)**

If you want to use the CHCP command to switch code pages for multiple foreign language character sets, invoke this command first. You need only invoke the command once per session; if you switch character sets often, place this command in the AUTOEXEC.BAT file.

The NLSFUNC command may be invoked without parameters. If you do so, DOS uses the country-specific information found in the COUNTRY.SYS file to support code page switching between international character sets using the CHCP command.

If you are using a file other than COUNTRY.SYS, or if COUNTRY.SYS cannot be found along the DOS search path, specify the correct file name and search path on the command line when you invoke NLSFUNC.

• EXAMPLES

NLSFUNC C:\SYS\COUNTRY.SYS

loads national language support functions from COUNTRY.SYS, located in the C:\SYS subdirectory.

• USING THE DOS 5.0 SHELL   The standard DOS shell is not
configured to invoke the NLSFUNC command. If you want, you can add the command to the Disk Utilities window. See Part 3, "The DOS Shell," for details on changing the display and adding commands.

• NOTES   If you are using DOS versions 4.0+, you can use the
INSTALL command in CONFIG.SYS to install NLSFUNC. See Appendix B, "CONFIG.SYS Commands," for details.

See Also   CHCP

PATH

I

2.0+

Specifies a list of subdirectories (the *search path*) where DOS is to look for executable program files.

• SYNTAX

PATH (*drive*:\ *path* ; *drive*:\ *path* ; ...)

If invoked without parameters, PATH displays the current search path, if any.

If you want to create or change the search path, invoke PATH followed by a list of the drives and subdirectories where you want DOS to look for program files. Drive letters must be followed by colons. Subdirectory names must be preceded by a backslash (\).

If you do not include a drive letter, DOS will assume that the subdirectory is on the currently logged drive. Otherwise, it always looks for the subdirectory on the specified drive.

The various locations included in the search path must be separated from the others by a semicolon (;).

The desired search path (including the PATH command to initialize it) can be a maximum of 127 characters long.

• EXAMPLES

PATH

displays the search path, or the message "No path" if not found. PATH; clears all search-path settings and instructs DOS to search only the current directory.

PATH C:\DOS;C:\WORD;C:\LOTUS;C:\SYS;C:\

instructs DOS to look for program files on the subdirectories \DOS, \WORD, \LOTUS, \SYS, and the root directory, all on drive C.

PATH \DOS;\WORD;\LOTUS;\SYS;\

instructs DOS to look for program files on the same set of subdirectories as the previous example; however, DOS will look for them on whatever drive is currently logged.

• ERROR MESSAGES

Invalid path

You have exceeded the limit of 63 characters in your path name. Try using SUBST to assign a drive letter to your longer subdirectory paths, and include the assigned drive letter instead.

No path

You have not initialized a search path. Re-invoke the path command and supply the desired search path on the command line.

● **USING THE DOS 5.0 SHELL**   If you set up a search path in AUTOEXEC.BAT before you run the shell, you may select File from the menu bar, then select Run and enter the name of a program file. If the file is on the search path, DOS will run the program.

The standard DOS shell has no provision for setting the search path, but you can locate individual program files by selecting a drive letter from the drive display, then selecting File from the menu bar. Select Search from the File menu and enter the name of the program file you want. You may use wildcard characters if you like. DOS will search the current disk for the program file. If it finds the file, it will display its name and location. Click twice on the displayed program file name, or press Enter, and DOS will run the program.

You may use this search technique to locate any file on the currently logged disk.

● **NOTES**   The PATH command creates a search path for program files only. Program files are files with extensions .EXE, .COM, or .SYS. To create a search path for data files in DOS versions 3.3+, use the APPEND command.

See Also   APPEND

PRINT

E

2.0+

▌ TSR

Sets aside a portion of RAM to be used for printing a series of files in the background while you continue to work with DOS.

● SYNTAX

PRINT (/*options*) (*drive*:\ *path*\ *file(s)*) (/*options*)

If invoked without parameters, PRINT displays the status of the print *queue* (the list of files to be printed).

To configure DOS for background printing, enter the PRINT command followed by whatever options you desire (or none if the default values are acceptable) and a file name. Wildcard characters are permitted in file names. Each time you invoke PRINT with file names, the files are added to the print queue, up to the maximum specified by the /Q switch (see the Options section). DOS sends the contents of the file to a buffer in RAM, which in turn sends the data to the printing device, while allowing you to continue to invoke other operating system commands or application software.

Each file name, including its subdirectory location, may be up to 64 characters long.

● OPTIONS

When background printing is active, DOS is alternating very quickly between the foreground processing and the background printing. Optional parameters allow you to control which output device receives the output, how memory is split between printing and processing, how to allocate the time spent on each, and the maximum number of files that may be lined up for printing.

The /D switch, if used, must be first on the command line after the PRINT command. The /D, /B, /U, /M, /S, and /Q switches configure the background printing environment; therefore, they may be used only once per session, the first time you invoke PRINT. The /C and /P switches must be preceded by a file name. All switches may be followed by file names, except the /Q switch, which may not be used on the same command line with a file name.

The least confusing way to use the PRINT command is to invoke it once with the configuration switches, then a second time to add file names to the queue.

/B:*buffer size*	Specifies the size, in bytes, of the printer buffer. Default is 512 bytes. The maximum size is 16,384 bytes. A larger buffer speeds printing, but requires additional RAM that may be needed by other commands.
/D:*device*	Specifies the output device name. If you do not use this switch on the command line (it must be the first switch following PRINT), DOS will prompt you to enter the device name. Default is PRN, the first parallel port on your system. Other possible output device names are LPT1 through LPT3, or COM1 though COM4. Do not use a colon following the device name.
/M:*ticks*	Specifies the maximum number of internal clock ticks DOS will take to send a character to the printer. Default is 2. The maximum value is 255.
/Q:*queue size*	Specifies the maximum number of files allowed in the print queue. The minimum number of files is 4, the maximum is 32. Default is 10.
/S:*slice*	Specifies the maximum number of internal clock ticks DOS will allow for foreground processing. Default is 8. The maximum value is 255.
/T	Removes all files from the print queue.
/U:*ticks*	Specifies the number of ticks on the computer's internal clock that DOS will wait before giving up and returning to foreground processing if the printer is not ready to receive data. Default is 1.
file name /C	Removes the indicated file name from the print queue. If additional file names follow this switch, they are removed as well.

file name /P Adds the indicated file name to the print queue. If additional file names follow this switch, they are added to the queue also.

● EXAMPLES

PRINT /D:COM1 /Q:32 /B:4096 /S:20 /M:4 /U:2

directs the printing output to the first serial port, allows 32 file names in the print queue, sets a buffer size of 4Kb, sets the foreground processing time to 20 clock ticks, sets the background printing time to 4 clock ticks, and waits for 2 ticks if the printer is busy.

PRINT C:\REPORT*.TXT

prints all files in the C:\REPORT subdirectory with the .TXT extension.

PRINT C:\REPORT\REPORT3.TXT /C
C:\REPORT\REPORT3.BAK /P

removes C:\REPORT\REPORT3.TXT from the print queue and adds C:\REPORT\REPORT3.BAK to the print queue.

● ERROR MESSAGES

Cannot use PRINT

You cannot use the PRINT command over a network. Use a separate non-DOS printing utility designed for your network instead.

File not in PRINT queue

You have attempted to remove a file from the queue that is no longer in the queue. If you have entered the file name correctly, the problem may be the result of using PRINT with a printer that has a large buffer.

List output is not assigned to a device

You entered an invalid device name when you invoked the PRINT command. Use a device name that is associated with a printer; for example, PRN, LPT1–3, or COM1–4.

Queue is full

You have attempted to exceed the maximum number of files allowed in the print queue. Wait for a file to be printed and try again. You may increase the default (10 files) using the /Q option.

● **USING THE DOS 5.0 SHELL** You must install PRINT before attempting to print from the DOS shell. To print from the DOS shell, do the following:

- If you want to print several files in different subdirectories, first select Options from the menu bar, then select Select across directories. A small dot will appear next to this option when it is active.

- To select a file, highlight the subdirectory in the Directory Tree window, then select the file name from the File Listing window. If you are selecting several files with the mouse, hold down the Control key while you select each file name. If you are using the keyboard and want to select several files, select the first by pressing Shift-F8. The word "Add" will appear in the lower-right corner of the screen. Then, move the highlight bar with the arrow keys, selecting each additional file by pressing the spacebar. Pressing Shift-F8 a second time will toggle this additional file mode off. The maximum number of files you may pick depends on what you specified with PRINT's /Q switch.

When all files are selected, select File from the menu bar, then select Print from the File pull-down menu. The files will print while you remain in the DOS shell.

● **NOTES** The PRINT utility only works from DOS. It has no effect on printing commands that are invoked from within other applications. It can print text files while other applications are running; depending on the specific application and the switch settings for PRINT, it may cause a noticeable reduction in processing speed.

Disk accessing interrupts background printing. Programs that access the disk frequently will degrade the performance of PRINT.

PROMPT

Changes the appearance of the DOS system prompt. Sends Escape codes to ANSI.SYS.

● SYNTAX

PROMPT (*prompt string*)

Using PROMPT without parameters will cause DOS to display its default system prompt, which is the letter of the currently logged drive followed by a greater-than symbol; for example, C>.

You may specify a custom prompt string, consisting of any character string you wish, and DOS will display the string as the system prompt.

Certain special effects characters may be added to the prompt string:

$_	Jumps down one line (for multiline prompts)
$$	Dollar sign ($)
$b	Piping symbol (¦)
$d	Current date
$e	ESC character
$g	Greater-than symbol (>)
$h	Backspace
$l	Less-than symbol (<)
$N	Current drive
$p	Currently logged drive and directory

$q   Equal sign (=)

$t   Current time

$v   DOS version number

If you have loaded the ANSI.SYS driver file in CONFIG.SYS, you may use the $e character to send Escape sequences for keyboard and cursor control to ANSI.SYS. See Appendix B, "CONFIG.SYS Commands," and Appendix C, "Standard MS-DOS Device Driver Files," for more details.

● EXAMPLES

PROMPT pg

sets the system prompt to include the currently logged subdirectory, followed by a greater-than symbol; for example: C:\DOS>.

PROMPT Please enter DOS command:$_$p$g

sets the system prompt to ask for command entry, and places the current path on the next line.

PROMPT $E[0;36;1;44m
PROMPT $E[2J
PROMPT pg

When the ANSI.SYS driver is loaded on a system with a color monitor, this sequence sets the screen to bright cyan text on a blue background, clears the screen, and displays the currently logged subdirectory in the DOS prompt. Refer to Appendix C for more details on using Escape codes in DOS commands.

● USING THE DOS 5.0 SHELL
Changes to the DOS prompt do not affect the performance of the DOS shell. However, any changes you make to the prompt before you enter the shell will be reflected in the appearance of the prompt in the shell if you call up the operating system by pressing Shift-F9.

● NOTES
The special effects characters in the prompt string are not case-sensitive; that is, they work in either upper- or lowercase. ANSI.SYS is case sensitive, however; be careful when sending Escape codes to ANSI.SYS.

RD OR RMDIR

| I |
| 2.0+ |

Removes empty subdirectories.

● SYNTAX

RMDIR (*drive:\path*) *subdirectory name*
RD (*drive:\path*) *subdirectory name*

RMDIR requires that you supply the name of a completely empty subdirectory, that is, a subdirectory that does not contain any files. You cannot remove the currently logged subdirectory. If the subdirectory that you want to remove is located on a different drive or nested below other subdirectories, you must include the full subdirectory path to the unwanted directory on the command line.

● EXAMPLES

RD OLDDIR

removes an empty subdirectory named OLDDIR located on a level just below the current subdirectory.

RD \OLDDIR

removes an empty subdirectory named OLDDIR located one level below the root directory on the currently logged drive.

RD C:\WORD\OLDDIR

removes an empty subdirectory named OLDDIR one level below the WORD subdirectory, which is just below the root directory on drive C.

● ERROR MESSAGES

Invalid path, not a directory, or directory not empty

You have attempted to remove a directory that contains files, or other subdirectories. Check the contents of the directory. If it appears completely empty, it may contain hidden files. Use the DIR command with the /A:H option to reveal these files.

● **USING THE DOS 5.0 SHELL**   To remove an empty directory, highlight the directory by picking the directory name from the Directory Tree window, and then press the Delete key. A dialog box appears, asking you to confirm that you intend to delete the directory.

If you are unable to delete what appears to be an empty directory, select the Options command from the menu bar, then select File display options. Select the check box to the left of the prompt, Display hidden/system files, then select the OK box. If hidden files appear in the directory, you must delete or move them before you can remove the directory.

● **NOTES**   Directories that contain hidden files may appear empty, but cannot be removed until the hidden files are deleted or moved from the directory. DOS offers no command-line options for viewing or manipulating hidden files, but you can make them visible in the DOS shell.

Some application software packages create hidden files. Some may be erased without problems; others are created as part of copy-protection schemes devised by software developers. Be very careful when manipulating hidden files; if you delete them, you may render your application software unusable. If you are in doubt regarding the purpose of any hidden files in your subdirectories, contact technical support for the software packages you are using.

You cannot remove your root directory.

See Also   CD, CHDIR, MD, MKDIR

RECOVER

| E |

| 2.0+ |

| ⊙ | Can overwrite or erase data!

Recovers files that have developed bad disk sector addresses by copying them, less the data that occupied the bad sectors, to a new location on disk. RECOVER also marks the bad sectors it finds so that further data will not be written to them.

● SYNTAX

RECOVER (drive:\path\) file name

RECOVER is normally used with a file name. Wildcard characters are accepted, but RECOVER will only work on the first file it finds that matches the file name specification.

If the disk directory is not usable, RECOVER may be used on an entire disk by specifying a drive letter instead of a file name. All files on the disk (including those in subdirectories) are copied to the root directory; they are given the name FILEnnnn.REC, where nnnn is a sequential number starting with 0000. If there are too many files on the disk to fit in the root directory, the remainder will be left unrecovered. You must delete some of the recovered files and repeat the process. This usage has potential for enormous disruption of files on a hard disk, so use this variation as a last resort only.

Be wary when using RECOVER with early versions of DOS. Some earlier versions of RECOVER allowed you to invoke the command without parameters, in which case it would recover all files on the currently logged disk drive, creating FILEnnnn.REC files.

● EXAMPLES

RECOVER REPORT.TXT

recovers the file REPORT.TXT and reports on the number of bytes DOS was able to copy to the new location.

RECOVER A:

recovers all the files on drive A.

● ERROR MESSAGES

Cannot RECOVER a network drive

You cannot use the RECOVER command on drives that have been redirected over a network.

Warning - directory full

DOS has run out of room on the target disk. Backup and delete some files to make room, and try again.

● USING THE DOS 5.0 SHELL   The standard DOS shell is not

configured to invoke the RECOVER command. If you want, you can add the command to the Disk Utilities window. See Part 3, "The DOS Shell," for details on changing the display and adding commands.

● NOTES   RECOVER is designed for the sole purpose of re-

covering files that have developed bad sectors. Do not use RECOVER to restore deleted files. If you are using DOS 5.0, use UNDELETE instead; with earlier versions, use a commercial utility program designed for this purpose. Do not use RECOVER to attempt to restore files made with the BACKUP command; use RESTORE instead.

Do not use RECOVER from a remote node on a network, or with drives that have been reassigned using the JOIN or SUBST commands.

REN OR RENAME

I
1.0+

Changes file names.

● SYNTAX

REN (drive\ path\ )old file name(s) new file name(s)

The REN command requires an old file name and a new file name. When invoked, the command changes the old name to the new. Wildcard characters may be used to rename groups of files, but the wildcard specification must match between the old name and new.

If the old file is not located in the current drive or subdirectory, you may specify the drive and path name as part of the old file name parameter. It is not necessary to repeat the drive and path names with the new file name; DOS will keep the renamed file in its original location.

● EXAMPLES

REN REPORT.TXT SALES.RPT

changes the name of REPORT.TXT to SALES.RPT.

REN C:\WORD*.BAK *.OLD

changes the names of all files with the extension .BAK on the C:\WORD subdirectory so that they now have the extension .OLD.

● USING THE DOS 5.0 SHELL   To rename files in the DOS

shell, first highlight their names in the current File List window. Then select File from the menu bar, followed by Rename. When the dialog box appears, enter the new file name for each of the new files.

See Also COPY

REPLACE

E

3.2+

| ⊙ | Can overwrite or erase data!
|---|

Selectively updates files on a target directory by replacing them with files of the same name on a source directory, or adds files to the target directory from the source.

● SYNTAX

REPLACE (*source drive*:\ *path*)*file(s) target drive*:(\ *path*) (/*options*)

REPLACE requires two parameters: source file names (wildcard characters are allowed) and a target drive, where the replacement files are to be copied. Source file names may include a drive letter and subdirectory path, and the target drive may include a subdirectory path as well. The target parameter does not include file names or wildcard characters.

REPLACE differs from the COPY command in that it is more flexible, allowing various optional approaches to the process of copying files from one location to another.

● OPTIONS

/A   Adds files. Copies files from the source only if they do not already exist on the target. This option may not be used with the /S or /U options.

/P   Displays a prompt asking you to confirm each copy before copying the file to the target.

/R   Disables overwrite protection for read-only files on the target.

/S   Searches all subdirectories of the target directory for files that match the name of each source file. Source subdirectories are not searched. Do not use this option with the /A option.

/U   Updates only: replaces files in the target location only if they are older than those in the source location.

/W   Pauses processing before starting the replacement process. Allows you to switch source or target disks if necessary.

● EXAMPLES

REPLACE A:*.* C: /S /U /P

replaces files on drive C (the target) that have the same name as any files on drive A (the source) only if those files on drive C are older than the files on drive A, and prompts for confirmation before each replacement is made.

● ERRORLEVEL CODES

0 = Replacement successful

2 = Source or target files not found

3 = Source or target locations not found

5 = Disk access denied; disk write-protect enabled

8 = Insufficient RAM to process command

11 = Syntax error on command line

15 = Invalid drive specification

• ERROR MESSAGES

No files added or replaced

REPLACE did not find any files that needed to be updated. Check your file specification and try again.

No files found

REPLACE found no files that matched your file specification parameter. Check the parameter and try again.

• USING THE DOS 5.0 SHELL   REPLACE cannot be invoked directly from the standard DOS shell. However, this is a handy command to add to the Disk Utilities window. See Part 3, "The DOS Shell," for details on changing the display and adding commands.

• NOTES   Do not use REPLACE to copy files from a source drive made using the BACKUP command. Use RESTORE instead.

See Also   COPY

RESTORE

E

2.0+

| ⊙ | Can overwrite or erase data!
|---|

Restores files from disks made using the BACKUP command.

● SYNTAX

RESTORE *source drive*: *target drive*:(\ *path*\ *file(s)*)
(/*options*)

RESTORE requires two parameters: a source drive (a floppy-disk drive), where the backup files are located, and a target drive (usually a hard disk), where the restored files are to be located.

RESTORE is used only to restore files that were backed up using the BACKUP command. BACKUP remembers the original subdirectory locations of the files it backs up, and RESTORE will attempt to restore the backup files to the same subdirectory. If the target subdirectory is not explicitly included on the command line, DOS assumes that the currently logged subdirectory is the target subdirectory. Therefore, before attempting to restore files to a subdirectory, be sure either to log onto that subdirectory before invoking RESTORE, or include the subdirectory path as part of the target parameter.

● OPTIONS

/A:*mm-dd-yy*   Forces restoration of only those files that were modified on or after the specified date, where *mm* is the month, *dd* is the day, and *yy* is the year. Files modified before the specified date are not restored.

/B:*mm-dd-yy*   Forces restoration of only those files that were modified on or before the specified date. Files modified after the specified date are not restored.

/D   Displays file name(s) on the backup disk but does not restore them.

/E:*hh-mm-ss*   Forces restoration of those files modified at or earlier than the specified time, where *hh* is the hour (in 24-hours format), *mm* is the minutes after the hour, and *ss* is the seconds. This switch is effective when used with the /B switch. Without a date parameter, target files from different dates can be overwritten if their time stamp matches the specified pattern.

/L:*hh:mm:ss*   Forces restoration of only those files that were modified at or after the specified time. Files modified before the specified time are not restored. Without a date parameter, target files from different dates can be overwritten if their time stamp matches the specified pattern.

/M   Restores only those files that were modified since the last backup was made.

/N   Restores only those files that were deleted since the last backup.

/P   Prompts to confirm the restoration of files that were changed since the last backup or marked as read-only files. Without this parameter, all files on the target drive with names identical to the backup files will be overwritten.

/S   Restores files in subdirectories nested below the specified target subdirectory (or the currently logged subdirectory if no target subdirectory was specified on the command line).

● EXAMPLES

RESTORE A: C:

restores those files from the backup disk in drive A that originally resided on the currently logged subdirectory.

RESTORE A: C:\ /S /B:06-01-91 /E:13:00:00 *

restores files from backup disk in drive A to the root directory of drive C, plus all files below the root directory, except those on the target drive that were modified on or after June 1, 1991, at 1:00 p.m.

● ERRORLEVEL CODES

0 = RESTORE command completed processing normally

1 = No files were found to restore

3 = Command terminated prematurely with Ctrl-C from operator

4 = Command terminated prematurely because of some internal error

● ERROR MESSAGES

*** Not able to restore file ***

The source or target disk may contain errors. Use the CHKDSK command to attempt to solve the problem. The disk may be unusable.

Warning! Disk is out of sequence

You are not restoring the backup disks in the same order in which you created them. You can disregard this message and press Enter, but some of your restored data files are likely to be corrupted. Make every effort to restore the disks in their original order.

Source does not contain backup files

DOS was unable to locate your specified source files. Check the subdirectory location and the file specification. Correct the syntax and try again.

Warning! No files were found to restore

Your file specification did not match files on the backup disk. Log onto the correct subdirectory, if possible. Review the command syntax carefully, and reenter the command with the correct file specification.

● **USING THE DOS 5.0 SHELL**   To restore backup files from
the DOS shell, click twice on Restore Fixed Disk in the DOS Utilities
window, or press Enter from the keyboard. If necessary, edit or add
the necessary command line parameters in the dialog box that appears on the screen. When the command parameters are correct,
select the OK button in the dialog box.

● **NOTES**   RESTORE can restore files that were backed up using
the same or earlier versions of DOS, but it cannot restore files that
were backed up using later versions of DOS. Check your DOS versions carefully if you are using BACKUP and RESTORE to move data
files between different computers.

See Also   BACKUP

SELECT

E

3.0+

| ⊙ | Can overwrite or erase data!

Installs DOS, or updates the current configuration by overwriting it.

● **SYNTAX**

For versions earlier than 4.0:

SELECT (*source drive:***) (***target drive:**path***) (***country***)**
(*keyboard***)**

If you specify a source drive, you must also specify a target drive,
and vice-versa. Only A or B are permitted as source drives. If you
omit the source and target drive parameters, A is used for the

source, B is used as the target. You may specify a subdirectory path for the target. If you do not specify a path, the root directory is used to hold the DOS files.

The *country* parameter is a 3-digit international font ID number taken from the COUNTRY.SYS file. This file must be present on the source drive if this parameter is used. If this parameter is omitted, the default is 001 (the ID number for the United States).

The *keyboard* is a two-letter international keyboard configuration code taken from the KEYBOARD.SYS file. This file must also be present on the source drive if this parameter is used. The default is US if this parameter is omitted.

Valid ID and keyboard codes are as follows:

Country	ID Number	Keyboard Code
United States	001	US
France	033	FR
Germany	049	GR
Italy	039	IT
Spain	034	SP
United Kingdom	044	UK

In versions 4.0+, the correct syntax is

SELECT

or you may place the installation disks in drive A and reboot using Ctrl-Alt-Del. You are taken through a series of instruction screens and menus that guide you through the DOS installation process. SELECT will permit you to indicate how memory is to be allocated between the operating system and application software, and to specify the country and keyboard configuration, default printer port, printer type, and various system optimizations. On each data entry screen, the default selection is highlighted. You may use the up and down arrow keys to highlight a different choice, and press Enter to accept the highlighted choice. If you would like help or further explanations, press F1.

Before invoking SELECT, you should know how much base memory your system has, how much additional memory in the form of expanded or extended memory it has, and whether you are using a serial or parallel printer.

● EXAMPLES

SELECT A: C:\DOS 044 UK

installs DOS version 3.x from drive A onto the C:\DOS subdirectory using the character font and keyboard configuration for the United Kingdom.

● ERROR MESSAGES

Failure to access COUNTRY.SYS

DOS was unable to locate the COUNTRY.SYS file. Make sure that the file is located on the source disk. If the file is corrupted, reinstall DOS from the master disks.

Failure to access KEYBOARD.SYS

DOS was unable to locate the KEYBOARD.SYS file. Make sure that the file is located on the source disk. If the file is corrupted, reinstall DOS from the master disks.

Invalid keyboard code

The specified keyboard code was not found in KEYBOARD.SYS. Correct the code and repeat the command.

Invalid signature

The KEYBOARD.SYS or COUNTRY.SYS files may have become corrupted. Reinstall DOS from the master disks.

Select error

The backup disk you are using may have become corrupted. Reinstall DOS from the master disks.

● USING THE DOS 5.0 SHELL   The standard DOS shell is

not configured to invoke the SELECT installation/configuration program. If you want, you can add the command to the Disk Utilities window. See Part 3, "The DOS Shell," for details on changing the display and adding commands.

● **NOTES** SELECT is intended to create new configurations of DOS. If you simply want to make bootable disks, the FORMAT /S command works more efficiently.

SELECT creates new CONFIG.SYS and AUTOEXEC.BAT files. If these files already exist on the target drive, DOS will prompt you to confirm that you want them overwritten. Often these two files are edited after DOS is installed. If you would like to preserve the contents of these files, respond affirmatively to the prompts that allow you to create copies of these files with the same name but a different file extension (depending on the DOS version). Later, you can use a text editor to combine the relevant commands from the two files.

SET

Creates environment variables and assigns values to them.

● **SYNTAX**

SET (*variable name*=) (*value*)

If you invoke the SET command without parameters, DOS displays a list of current environment variables and their values.

To initialize a variable or assign a new value to a variable, enter the name of a variable and an equal sign (=), followed by the desired value. The variable is stored in the operating system's *environment space,* an area of RAM set aside for this purpose. If the variable already exists in the environment, the value is changed to the indicated new value. If the variable does not already exist, it is created and assigned the value specified.

The environment space in DOS is limited. Refer to the SHELL command entry in Appendix B for details on changing the size of the environment space.

To remove a variable from the environment space, invoke SET with the variable name and equal sign, but do not indicate a value.

● EXAMPLES

SET COMSPEC=C:\DOS\COMMAND.COM

assigns the string C:\DOS\COMMAND.COM to an environment variable named COMSPEC. DOS uses this system variable to remember the location of the file COMMAND.COM.

● USING THE DOS 5.0 SHELL
You can create or change environment variables in the DOS shell by pressing Shift-F9 and invoking the SET command from the DOS prompt. However, because this DOS prompt is actually a secondary command processor, the values you assign, and possibly the variable names as well, will be valid only while you remain in the secondary processor; they will be lost entirely or returned to their original values when you invoke EXIT and return to the DOS shell.

All DOS commands that you invoke from the DOS shell operate within a secondary command processor, then return to the parent command processor running the shell. For this reason, there is no point in configuring the shell to create environment variables, since the values are immediately lost when the SET command is finished. To make use of environment variables from within the DOS shell, set them up using the SET command before invoking DOSSHELL, or perform whatever processing that uses the new values while you are still within the secondary command processor.

Alternatively, if you have enough RAM, you could press Shift-F9, change the values of environment variables using the SET command, then invoke the DOSSHELL command, in effect running the shell from within itself. This is a memory-intensive and potentially confusing technique. Use it only if there is no reasonable alternative.

● **NOTES** Many batch files and application software programs use environment variables. They can be quite handy. See Appendix A, "Using Batch Files," for examples of how environment variables can be used.

SETVER

E

5.0

Causes DOS to supply a different version number to an application.

● SYNTAX

SETVER *<drive:>* **application version** *</options>*

The SETVER command updates a table of applications that require DOS to provide an earlier version number. You must load this table into memory by including the command DEVICE=SETVER.EXE in your CONFIG.SYS file. Refer to Appendix C for details regarding this command in CONFIG.SYS.

To display the current table of applications, invoke SETVER without parameters. To add an application to the table, invoke SET-VER with the name of the application's executable file and the desired DOS version number. Thereafter, when you call that application, DOS will supply the specified version number rather than the current version. This is useful for programs that require an earlier version of DOS but can run under DOS 5.0.

• OPTIONS

/D   Deletes application names from the table.

/DELETE   Same as the /D option.

/Q   Suppresses on-screen messages when deleting
               applications from the table.

/QUIET   Same as the /Q option.

• EXAMPLES

SETVER MARIOZAP.EXE 3.3

instructs DOS to tell the MARIOZAP program that the DOS version
number is 3.3.

• ERROR MESSAGES

Insufficient space in version table

You have exceeded the maximum number of version entries. Delete
some of the entries and try again.

Invalid version number

You have specified a DOS version number that is out of range. Valid
ranges are from 3.20 to 9.99. Check your entry and try again.

Specified entry not found in the version table

You have attempted to delete an entry that DOS cannot find in the
version table. Correct the syntax and try again.

Version table is corrupt

Errors have developed in the version table. Delete entries if possible, and re-initialize. If necessary, reboot the computer and start
over. If the problem persists, it may indicate hardware problems;
have the computer serviced.

• USING THE DOS 5.0 SHELL   You can invoke the SETVER
command from within the DOS shell by pressing Shift-F9 and entering the command from the DOS prompt. Enter EXIT to return to the

shell. If you want, you can add the command to the Disk Utilities window. See Part 3, "The DOS Shell," for details on changing the display and adding commands.

● **NOTES**   Although the SETVER command will force DOS to provide a false version number, it does nothing to change the operating system's functioning. In other words, SETVER does not force DOS to act like an earlier version, but only to report that number. If an application requires exact version compatibility, you must use that version of DOS.

See Also   VER

SHARE

E

3.0+

TSR

Enables support for file sharing and locking.

● **SYNTAX**

SHARE (/*options*)

SHARE is normally used on network systems, where the same application and data files may by used simultaneously. It prevents open disk files from being overwritten in ways that might compromise their integrity.

For example, if you open a file on a floppy disk, then switch disks before closing the file, SHARE displays an error message and temporarily suspends processing until you return the original disk to the drive.

If the SHARE command is invoked without option switches, default values for these switches are used.

In versions 4.0+, you can also load the SHARE program using the INSTALL command in CONFIG.SYS. (See Appendix B, "CONFIG.SYS Commands.")

● OPTIONS

/F:*nnnn*   Allocates space in RAM to be used to store the names of open disk files, where *nnnn* is the size of the storage space in bytes. The default is 2048 bytes.

/L:*nn*   Indicates the number of files that can be opened and locked at the same time. A file is locked when it is opened for reading or writing, and cannot be accessed until it is closed again. The default is 20 locked files.

● EXAMPLES

SHARE /F:4096 /L:32

activates the SHARE program, allocates 4096 bytes for file name space, and allows a maximum of 32 locked files.

● ERROR MESSAGES

SHARE already installed

SHARE is already resident in memory. There is no need to install it again.

Sharing violation

You have attempted to open a file that was already open. This usually happens on a network, but can occur in other circumstances—for example, if you attempt to print and edit a file at the same time. Wait until the file is closed, then try to access it again.

● **USING THE DOS 5.0 SHELL**   If you intend to use SHARE
and the DOS shell, you should load it from the DOS prompt or batch
file before entering the shell. SHARE is a terminate-and-stay-resident program that should not be loaded from a secondary command
processor.

● **NOTES**   If you are using DOS version 4.0 or later and have
configured your hard drive to include partitions that are larger than
32Mb, SHARE is automatically loaded at boot time to assist DOS in
handling the temporary files it creates to handle large disk partitions.

SHARE can also help prevent temporary files created by extended
or expanded memory managers from conflicting with those created
by application programs. Check the documentation for your
memory manager and application software to determine if they
recommend using SHARE.

SORT

```
  E
 2.0+
```

Sorts data in character-based files, or sorts the output of DOS
commands.

● **SYNTAX**

SORT (/*options***) < (***drive***:\ ***path***\ )***file(s)*
command* (parameter(s)***) ¦ SORT (/***options***)**

The SORT command will produce character-based output in
numeric or alphabetical order. It arranges individual lines in text
files, or each line of output. It is intended to be used on data lists

(such as file directories or name lists) in which each line of the file contains some significant piece of information.

There are two ways to use the SORT command:

- If you would like to sort the contents of a data file, enter SORT followed by the redirection symbol for input (<) and the input file name. Wildcard characters are not allowed. SORT cannot handle files larger than 63Kb. SORT reads the file, sorts the lines, and displays the output. To redirect the output to another file, use the greater-than sign (>) followed by the output file name.

- If you would like to display the output of another command, enter the command and any required parameters followed by the redirection symbol for piping (¦) and SORT. You may also direct the command output that has been filtered through SORT to a file using the greater-than sign (>) and an output file name.

• OPTIONS

/R   Sorts in reverse order (Z to A, 9 to 0)

/+nn   Sorts using a character offset from the start of each line, where nn is the number of characters from the beginning

• EXAMPLES

SORT /R /+21 < NAMES.LST > RALPHA.LST

reads the file NAMES.LST, sorts it in reverse order on the 21st character of each line, and writes the result into a file named RAL-PHA.LST.

DIR ¦ SORT

sorts the output of the DIR command and displays the directory in alphabetical order.

• USING THE DOS 5.0 SHELL   SORT can be added to commands that you install in the DOS shell's program window. There

are a number of sorting options within the shell for the file name window. To change the order of the file name display, select Options from the menu bar, then select File display options. A dialog box will offer you the choice of sorting by name, extension, date, size, or disk order. All sorting options may be listed in reverse order by clicking on the box to the left of the Descending order prompt. If you are using the keyboard, highlight the prompt and press the spacebar.

● **NOTES**   In versions 3.0+, SORT is not case-sensitive—that is, all letters are treated as if uppercase. Earlier versions sorted upper-case letters before lowercase ones.

Characters that are not alphanumeric will be sorted according to their ASCII table value. These values can differ among international character font sets.

SUBST

E

3.1+

TSR

Associates a drive letter with a subdirectory path. Drive letters used this way are called *virtual drives*.

● **SYNTAX**

SUBST *new drive*: (*drive:*)\ *existing path* (/D)

SUBST allows you to use a drive letter as a substitute for a long sub-directory path name, saving you keystrokes. SUBST can also allow programs that do not recognize subdirectory paths to use them anyway via virtual drives. Because SUBST uses a single drive letter for a long subdirectory path, it can also be used to extend the PATH and APPEND command parameters past their normal limits.

SUBST requires that you specify the drive letter that you want to use in place of the subdirectory path name. This drive letter cannot refer to any existing drive letter in your system. The highest default drive letter you can use is E. To use a drive letter higher than E, add the LASTDRIVE command to your CONFIG.SYS file. If you have added the LASTDRIVE command to CONFIG.SYS, you can use any drive letter up to and including the drive letter specified by LASTDRIVE. See Appendix B, "CONFIG.SYS Commands," for details.

The subdirectory path must already exist, and if the drive letter is different from the currently logged drive, it must be specified as part of the existing path parameter.

● OPTIONS

/D   Deletes a drive letter that has been initialized with SUBST. Do not use the subdirectory path parameter with this switch.

● EXAMPLES

SUBST D: C:\WORD\USER\RUDOLPH

allows use of drive D in place of C:\WORD\USER\RUDOLPH in all commands that reference this subdirectory.

SUBST D: /D

After invoking the previous example, this command deletes drive D as a substitute for C:\WORD\USER\RUDOLPH.

● ERROR MESSAGES

Cannot SUBST a network drive

You cannot use the SUBST command on drives that have been redirected over a network.

● **USING THE DOS 5.0 SHELL**   The SUBST command, like all terminate-and-stay-resident commands, should be invoked outside of the DOS shell.

● **NOTES**   The following DOS commands will not work on drive letters that have been initialized using the SUBST command: ASSIGN, BACKUP, CHKDSK, DISKCOMP, DISKCOPY, FDISK, FORMAT, JOIN, LABEL, RECOVER, RESTORE, SYS.

The following DOS commands can work differently after SUBST is invoked, and should be used with care to avoid confusion: APPEND, CD, CHDIR, MD, MKDIR, PATH, RD, RMDIR.

See Also   ASSIGN, JOIN

SYS

E

1.0+

Copies DOS system files to a new disk.

● **SYNTAX**

For versions earlier than 4.0:

SYS *target drive*:

For versions 4.0 and later:

SYS *source drive*: *target drive*:

SYS transfers two operating system files to a formatted disk without requiring reformatting. These files must be located contiguously on the disk's first track and sector, or *boot sector*, so that the disk may be bootable, or capable of loading DOS at boot up. In addition to these system files, a disk must also contain the COM-MAND.COM file to be bootable. In DOS versions earlier than 5.0, SYS does not copy this file. You must copy it using the COPY command after invoking SYS. The FORMAT /S command also copies the system files, and copies COMMAND.COM as well.

In versions prior to 4.0, the source drive for the system files was always the currently logged drive. As of version 4.0, you can specify the source drive on the command line.

In versions prior to 4.0, system files were required to be *contiguous* (occupying adjacent sectors). If other files had been copied to the disk, they might occupy sectors required by the system files, in which case SYS would not be able to copy the system files. This would result in the message "No room for system on destination disk." To get the system files onto the disk, you must delete files on the disk to make room for the system files. Back up the disk, then either erase all the files and invoke SYS or FORMAT /S.

● EXAMPLES

SYS A:

copies system files to the disk in drive A.

SYS C: A:

copies system files to drive A from drive C, even if you are not logged onto drive C.

● ERROR MESSAGES

Cannot specify default drive

The SYS command could not recognize the drive letter you specified. Use a different drive letter.

Cannot SYS to a network drive

You cannot use the SYS command on drives that have been redirected over a network.

No room for system on destination disk

Other files are occupying the system file area of the target disk. If possible, back up and delete the current system files, plus the first few files that appear in an unsorted directory listing, then try the command again. If this does not work, you may have to reformat the disk using FORMAT with the /S option.

● **USING THE DOS 5.0 SHELL** The standard DOS shell is not configured to invoke the SYS command. If you want, you can add the command to the Disk Utilities window. See Part 3, "The DOS Shell," for details on changing the display and adding commands.

● **NOTES** SYS does not work on drives that have been reassigned using the JOIN or SUBST commands, nor will it work on a network.

See Also FORMAT /S

TIME

I
1.1+

Displays and allows changes to the system time.

● **SYNTAX**

TIME (*hh:mm:ss.cc*)(A)/(P)

If you invoke TIME without parameters, it displays the current system time and prompts you to enter a new time. If you do not want to change the current time, press Enter. Otherwise, enter the new time using the format as shown on the command line above, where *hh* is the hour of the day in 24-hour format, *mm* is the minutes after the hour, *ss* is the seconds after the minute, and *cc* is hundredths of a second. Only the hours parameter (followed by a colon) is required to set a new time; other time values are optional.

If you include the desired time on the command line, the system time is changed without prompting you.

In DOS 5.0, time can be entered in twelve-hour format. When entering a.m. time, use the letter *a*. When entering p.m. time, use the letter *p*.

● EXAMPLES

TIME 10:

changes the system time to 10:00 a.m.

TIME 22:30
TIME 10:30p

changes the system time to 10:30 p.m.

● ERROR MESSAGES

Invalid time

DOS cannot recognize the time format you have entered. Check your entry and try again.

● USING THE DOS 5.0 SHELL   The TIME command is not invoked from within the standard DOS shell, but the command could be added to the shell in the program window. See Part 3, "The DOS Shell," for details on changing the display and adding commands.

TREE

E

2.0+

Displays the subdirectory structure of a drive.

● SYNTAX

TREE (*drive:\path*) (*/options*)

If you invoke TREE without parameters, the subdirectory structure of the current drive is displayed. If you include a drive letter, the structure of the specified drive is displayed. If you include a subdirectory name, the structure starting at the specified subdirectory is displayed.

● OPTIONS

/F   Includes the file names in each subdirectory.

/A   Displays the subdirectory using standard ASCII characters rather than graphic characters; this can speed up printing.

● EXAMPLES

TREE ¦ MORE

displays the subdirectory structure of the currently logged drive, and pauses the screen display after each screenful of information.

TREE C: /F /A > PRN

displays the subdirectory structure of drive C, includes the file names in each subdirectory, and sends the output to the standard printing device in ASCII format.

● **USING THE DOS 5.0 SHELL**   To display the subdirectory structure in the Directory Tree, press Ctrl-* (asterisk). Alternatively, select Tree from the menu bar, then select Expand all.

● **NOTES**   The output from the TREE command can easily scroll off the screen, even when the subdirectory structure is relatively simple. For this reason, TREE's output is often redirected to a printer or a disk file, or piped through the MORE command. See the sections "Piping" and "Redirecting Output" in Part 1 and the MORE entry for more details.

TRUENAME

```
| I  |
| 4.0+ |
```

Displays the correct drive and subdirectory path names of drives and subdirectories that have been reassigned using the ASSIGN, JOIN, and SUBST commands.

● **SYNTAX**

TRUENAME (*drive*:) (\ *path*)

When invoked without parameters, TRUENAME displays the correct name of the currently logged drive and subdirectory. When invoked with a drive letter, TRUENAME reports the true name of the current subdirectory of the specified drive. When invoked with a subdirectory parameter, TRUENAME reports the correct name of the specified path.

● EXAMPLES

TRUENAME E:

reports the drive and subdirectory path assigned to drive E.

● USING THE DOS 5.0 SHELL
The standard DOS shell is not configured to invoke the TRUENAME command. If you want, you can add the command to the Disk Utilities window. See Part 3, "The DOS Shell," for details on changing the display and adding commands.

See Also   ASSIGN, JOIN, SUBST

TYPE

I

1.0+

Displays the contents of a file.

● SYNTAX

TYPE (*drive:\path*) *file*

TYPE requires the name of a file. You may include a drive and subdirectory name if the file is not on the currently logged drive and subdirectory. Wildcard characters are not allowed in the file name.

● EXAMPLES

TYPE REPORT.TXT

displays the contents of a file named REPORT.TXT on the screen.

TYPE REPORT.TXT ¦ MORE

displays the contents of the file and pauses the display after each screenful of information.

TYPE REPORT.TXT > PRN

sends the contents of REPORT.TXT to the standard printing device.

● **USING THE DOS 5.0 SHELL**   To view the contents of a disk file on the screen, first highlight the file you want to view in the File Display window, then press the F9 function key. Alternatively, after highlighting the file, you can pick File from the menu bar, followed by View file contents from the pull-down menu.

● **NOTES**   The TYPE command is intended to view ASCII text files. Program files and files created with many word processing programs may contain non-ASCII text characters, and thus will not be readable using the TYPE command.

If the file displayed by TYPE is too large, it can scroll off the screen. For this reason, the output from TYPE is often redirected to a printer or piped through the MORE command. See the sections "Piping" and "Redirecting Output" in Part 1 and the MORE entry for more details.

UNDELETE

E

5.0

Recovers accidentally deleted files.

● SYNTAX

UNDELETE (drive\path) file(s) (/options)

Invoke UNDELETE with the name of a deleted file. You may use wildcard characters to recover groups of files. If you omit a file name, UNDELETE will attempt to recover all the deleted files it finds.

For best results, invoke UNDELETE before any other information is written to the disk. Subsequent disk writes may overwrite the disk area occupied by the deleted file, making recovery impossible.

If you do not include a drive or subdirectory path before the file name, the currently logged drive and subdirectory are used.

UNDELETE displays each deleted file it finds that matches the specification in the command line. It prompts you to reenter the first character in the file name, which was lost when the file was deleted. After you enter the characters, UNDELETE attempts to recover the file.

● OPTIONS

/DT   Forces DOS to use a delete tracking file to locate and recover deleted files. This file is not created by DOS. If you do not have software that can create a delete tracking file, do not use this switch.

/DOS   Uses the DOS file directory to locate and recover deleted files. This is the default.

/LIST   Lists all deleted files that may be recoverable.

/ALL   Invokes automatic undeleting and renaming of all specified files. Processing takes place automatically without prompts to the user to rename files. Files are renamed using numbers as the first character, and letters if numbers create duplicate file names.

● EXAMPLES

UNDELETE *.BAK /LIST

lists all deleted files with the extension .BAK on the currently logged drive and subdirectory.

UNDELETE C:\WORD*.BAK

attempts to recover all files in the C:\WORD subdirectory that have the extension .BAK.

● USING THE DOS 5.0 SHELL   The standard DOS shell is
not configured to invoke the UNDELETE command. If you want, you can add the command to the Disk Utilities window. See Part 3, "The DOS Shell," for details on changing the display and adding commands. On some systems, more reliable results may be obtained by running UNDELETE from the DOS prompt.

● NOTES   Do not redirect the output of UNDELETE to a disk
file. You may overwrite the files you are attempting to recover.

The results of using UNDELETE will vary from system to system. It is intended for last-resort use only. This utility is not intended to be a substitute for making backup copies of your files.

See Also   UNFORMAT

UNFORMAT

E

5.0

Recovers files from an accidental disk format.

• SYNTAX

UNFORMAT *drive*: (/*options*)

If a disk has been accidentally formatted, you may be able to recover files on it by invoking UNFORMAT (from a floppy disk, if your hard disk was reformatted), followed by the drive letter for the formatted disk. In order for UNFORMAT to work most reliably, you should have previously saved an image of the file allocation table (FAT) and root directory using the MIRROR command. If you have not saved the image file, UNFORMAT may still restore some or all of the files on your disk, although it is much less reliable under these circumstances.

• OPTIONS

The following switches are for use when an image file was saved using the MIRROR command:

/J	Compares the system area with the saved image; does not rebuild the disk.
/PARTN	Restores the saved disk partition table; you must have previously used the /PARTN switch when you invoked the MIRROR command.
/L	Lists the existing partitions, but does not restore them. Use this switch with the /PARTN switch.
/U	Restores the disk without using the image file.

The following switches may be used when you did not previously create an image file using the MIRROR command:

/L	Lists any file names found on the formatted drive
/TEST	Processes but does not write any changes to the formatted disk
/P	Echoes program messages to the standard printing device

● EXAMPLES

UNFORMAT C:

restores an accidentally reformatted disk in drive C.

UNFORMAT C: /TEST /L

tests recovery chances on a formatted disk in drive C when a FAT data file does not exist and lists file names found.

● USING THE DOS 5.0 SHELL   Because UNFORMAT reconstructs file allocation tables, it is not recommended that you run this utility from the DOS shell. Run UNFORMAT from the DOS prompt; do not load any terminate-and-stay-resident software before invoking this command.

● NOTES   The results of UNFORMAT will vary from system to system. It is intended for last-resort use only. It is not an adequate substitute for backing up your data.

See Also   MIRROR, UNDELETE

VER

I

2.0+

Displays the current DOS version number.

● SYNTAX

VER

The VER command displays the current DOS version. VER has no additional parameters or option switches.

● **USING THE DOS 5.0 SHELL** To display the current DOS version from the shell, select Help from the menu bar, then select About shell from the pull-down menu.

VERIFY

I

2.0+

Enables/disables the verify switch for writing files during DOS operations.

● **SYNTAX**

VERIFY (on) (off)

If invoked without parameters, VERIFY displays the current state of the verify switch. Otherwise, invoke VERIFY using either the *on* or *off* parameter.

When the verify switch is on, DOS compares the image of a file just written to a disk with the image of that file in memory. DOS will display an error message if it is unable to write a verifiable copy of the file. When the verify switch is off, no such comparison is made. The default setting for the verify switch is off.

● **EXAMPLES**

VERIFY ON

turns on the verify switch.

● **USING THE DOS 5.0 SHELL**   You can change the setting of the verify switch in the DOS shell by pressing Shift-F9 and invoking the VERIFY ON or OFF command from the DOS prompt. The changes you make will remain valid after you invoke EXIT and return to the DOS shell. If you want, you can add the command to the Disk Utilities window. See Part 3, "The DOS Shell," for details on changing the display and adding commands.

● **NOTES**   Setting the verify switch on has the same effect on COPY commands as the /v option switch. Including this switch in COPY's command line overrides a verify off setting for the duration of the COPY command.

VERIFY has some limitations. The copy is compared to the image of the file in RAM, not the original file on disk. Thus, VERIFY will not discover any error that occurred while the original file was being read into RAM. The verification mechanism is a cyclic redundancy check, which only verifies that DOS wrote something to the disk. It is not a byte-by-byte comparison. To perform a more complete comparison of the file copy with the original, use the COMP or FC commands.

VOL

```
  I
2.0+
```

Displays the disk volume label.

● **SYNTAX**

VOL (*drive*:)

If invoked without parameters, VOL displays the currently logged drive volume label, if any. If you include the drive letter parameter, that drive's volume label is displayed. In versions 4.0 and later, the disk serial number is displayed as well.

● EXAMPLES

VOL A:

displays the volume label in drive A.

● USING THE DOS 5.0 SHELL   To view the volume label from the shell, highlight the drive in the drive display. Select Options from the menu bar, then select Show information. A window appears, showing information about the current file and disk. The volume label appears after the Name heading.

See Also   FORMAT /V, LABEL

XCOPY

E

3.2+

Selectively copies files.

● SYNTAX

XCOPY (*source drive*:\ *path*) *source file(s)* (*target drive*:\ *path*) *target file(s)* (/ *options*)

At a minimum, the XCOPY command requires a source file name, which may include wildcard characters, plus optional drive letter and subdirectory path. You may provide a target parameter as well, which may be another file name, drive letter, subdirectory path, or a combination of the three. If you do not include a target, XCOPY will attempt to copy the source files onto the currently logged drive and subdirectory.

The source and target parameters may not duplicate the same file name and location. In other words, the XCOPY command will not copy a file onto itself.

If you use wildcard characters to indicate multiple source files and the target does not include a file name, copies of each file matching the source specification will be made in the target location.

If you indicate multiple source files and the target file name also includes wildcard characters, DOS will attempt to rename the target files in accordance with the wildcard conventions that you indicate. For predictable results, keep the wildcard character specifications consistent between the source and target file names.

● OPTIONS

The available options make XCOPY more flexible than the COPY command.

/A	Copies only those files matching the source specification that also have their archive bit set. See the ATTRIB entry for details about setting the archive bit.
/D:*mm*/*dd*/*yy*	Copies files that were modified on or after the specified date.
/E	Creates subdirectories on the target location, even if there are no files in them. This switch is valid only when used in conjunction with the /S switch.
/M	Resets (turns off) the archive bit in a file after making the copy.
/P	Issues a prompt asking you to confirm the copy of each source file.
/S	Copies files matching the source specification that are found in subdirectories nested below the source subdirectory.

| /V | Performs a CRC verification check against the image of the file in memory. |
| /W | Causes XCOPY to pause before making copies, allowing you an opportunity to change disks in the source drive if necessary. |

• EXAMPLES

XCOPY C:\REPORTS*.TXT B:

copies all files in the C:\REPORTS subdirectory with the extension .TXT to drive B.

XCOPY C:\REPORTS*.TXT B: /S /D:06/01/91

copies all files in the C:\REPORTS subdirectory, as well as any located in subdirectories nested below C:\REPORTS, with the extension .TXT, provided that they have been modified on or after June 1, 1991. The copies are placed on drive B.

• ERRORLEVEL CODES

0 = Copies made successfully

1 = No files found matching the source specification

2 = XCOPY aborted by operator (Ctrl-C)

4 = Invalid syntax on the command line, or insufficient memory to run XCOPY

5 = Disk error encountered reading or writing files

• ERROR MESSAGES

Cannot perform a cyclic copy

You have attempted to copy files onto themselves. This can happen when you have used the /S option, and are attempting to copy to a subdirectory nested below the source subdirectory.

Cannot XCOPY to a reserved device

You have entered an invalid target parameter. Specify a file or disk drive as your target, and re-invoke the command.

● **USING THE DOS 5.0 SHELL**   The standard DOS shell is not configured to invoke the XCOPY command. If you want, you can add the command to the Disk Utilities window. See Part 3, "The DOS Shell," for details on changing the display and adding commands.

You can copy groups of files from the shell. If you wish to copy files from several different subdirectories, first select Options from the menu bar, then select Select across directories from the pull-down menu. This will allow you to change directories without losing files you have already selected.

Select the desired files from the list in the File List window. Then, press the F8 key, or select the File pull-down menu, followed by Copy. A dialog box will appear, indicating the chosen file(s) and the new destination. To change the currently displayed destination, re-type a new one. If you would like to edit the current destination, press the right or left arrow key before typing any characters. If you wish to change the source listing, press Esc and choose different files from the display window.

When you have entered the desired destination, press Enter or select the OK box, and the files will be copied.

Copying several files from the shell is not as fast as using XCOPY with wildcard file specifications. To invoke XCOPY directly, press Shift-F9 and invoke the XCOPY command from the DOS prompt. When finished, enter EXIT to return to the shell.

● **NOTES**   In addition to being more flexible than BACKUP or COPY, XCOPY can handle large numbers of files more efficiently, because it reads as many files as it can into memory before writing them to disk. This lessens the number of disk accesses. If you copy lots of smaller files, this can save you time and reduce disk wear and tear.

If you use the /A and /M option switches, XCOPY can copy a group of files that might not fit on a single floppy disk. Wait for the disk to fill up, replace it with a new disk, and restart XCOPY by pressing F3. Because the /A switch instructs XCOPY to copy only files with the archive bit set and the /M switch updates the archive bit after each file is copied, the earlier copies will not be included on subsequent floppy disks.

XCOPY has some advantages over DISKCOPY: fragmented source files will be de-fragmented on the target disk, and XCOPY can copy files between disks with different data capacities. However, XCOPY cannot format disks on the fly as DISKCOPY can.

See Also   COPY, BACKUP

Part 3

The DOS Shell

DOS's abstract line commands and its minimal prompting use computer resources efficiently; however, this approach often forces the user to memorize arcane commands and parameters. Many users are comfortable with DOS's line command and C prompt; other users who would rather work in a more concrete and intuitive environment will appreciate an important new feature that first appeared in DOS 4.0 and has been greatly expanded in version 5.0: a graphic user interface called the *DOS shell*.

The DOS shell allows you to perform a wide variety of everyday file management tasks in a more intuitive way. For example, you can

- Maintain an ongoing display of your hard disk's subdirectory structure plus lists of files within each subdirectory.
- Launch an application program by pointing to a data file you have associated with it.
- Move, copy, and delete data files in a graphic, menu-driven context.

In addition to these more traditional tasks, the DOS shell allows you to do some things that are impossible at the DOS prompt:

- Maintain and switch between more than one open application program at a time.
- Display multiple disks or subdirectories.
- Rename subdirectories without copying and deleting files.
- Customize the look and feel of your working environment.

This chapter discusses the shell's features and provides a reference to its standard command set.

THE SHELL DISPLAY

Load the DOS shell by invoking **DOSSHELL** at the DOS prompt. If you plan to use the DOS shell frequently, you may want to include the command as the last line in your AUTOEXEC.BAT file. After you invoke the command you will see a display similar to the one pictured in Figure 3.1.

The following sections describe the main features of the shell and how to use them.

THE POINTER

The *pointer* is a small icon that moves about the screen. You control its movements by means of a peripheral device such as a *mouse* (which tracks your hand movement while you hold it), a *trackball* (a ball that records movement as you rotate it in place), or by means of

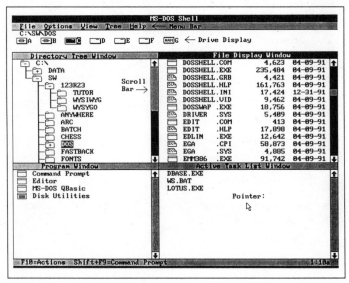

Figure 3.1: The DOS shell

the arrow keys on the keyboard. Although all the features of the DOS shell are accessible by means of the keyboard, this is the least efficient means of using the shell, and a mouse or trackball is recommended. For the sake of simplicity, this text refers to any tracking device as a mouse.

A mouse includes at least one button, called the *pick button.* The DOS shell makes use of only this one button. If your mouse has more than one button, you may have to experiment with your device to determine which is the pick button.

You can use either the mouse or the keyboard to move the pointer between the various windows, select menu commands or file names, start applications, or change drives and subdirectories. If you are not using a mouse, you may use the Tab key to highlight different windows in sequential order, and use the keyboard's arrow keys to move the pointer between highlighted items in a selected window. You may select an item by pressing the spacebar or Enter.

HIGHLIGHTING AND SELECTING ITEMS

Several terms in this chapter are used frequently to refer to highlighting and selecting items in the DOS shell:

An item is *highlighted* when it appears in a different or reverse color. To highlight items, touch them with the pointer and press the pick button.

To *pick,* or *select,* an item, touch it with the pointer and press the pick button once. If you are using the keyboard, move the pointer using the keyboard's arrow keys and press the spacebar.

To *double-click* on an item, move the pointer to it and quickly press the pick button twice. To accomplish the same thing using the keyboard, move the pointer with the arrow keys and press Enter.

Refer to the section later in Part 3 entitled "File Display" for other techniques to use when picking file names.

In certain circumstances, you may need to move the mouse while holding the pick button down. For example, you use this technique to start applications with default files. To do this, first pick the default file. Then, while holding the pick button down, move the pointer to the application file name (a file with the extension .COM, .EXE, or .BAT). If the application can be successfully launched with the selected data file, the pointer icon will be replaced by the data file's icon. If the application cannot be successfully launched, the pointer arrow is replaced by a small circle with a diagonal line through the center.

Other examples of this technique can be found in the discussions of the Move and Copy commands later in Part 3.

THE MENU BAR

The *menu bar* is the first active line on the DOS shell screen. It contains *keywords* that activate pull-down menus of various operating system commands. These menus and their associated commands are described in more detail later in Part 3.

To activate a menu, highlight the associated keyword, then press the pick button. If you are using the keyboard, you may activate the pull-down menus by holding down the Alt key and pressing the first letter of the keyword. For example, to activate the File pull-down menu, press Alt-F. Alternatively, you may access the menu bar by pressing the F10 function key, and moving between the keywords using the arrow keys.

THE DRIVE DISPLAY

The *drive display* appears just under the menu bar. It shows which drives are available in the system. In the DOS shell's graphics display, the drives are represented by a drive letter followed by an *icon*, a small picture, that indicates the type of drive associated with each letter. If the drive is a floppy-disk drive, the drive icon includes a drive bay door. If the drive is a hard-disk drive, the icon does not include the door catch. If the drive is a RAM disk, the icon appears as a small memory chip. Refer to Figure 3.1 for an illustration of each of these icons.

To make a drive active, move the pointer to the desired drive letter and press the pick button. If you are using the keyboard, move the pointer using the keyboard's arrow keys, and press the spacebar.

THE DIRECTORY TREE

The *directory tree window* displays the subdirectory structure of the currently active drive. To log onto a particular subdirectory, move the pointer to it and select it.

Each subdirectory is accompanied by an icon that looks like a little file folder. If there are subdirectories nested below a given subdirectory, the icon will contain a small plus symbol (+). You may display these nested subdirectories by picking the icon. If you are using the keyboard, highlight the subdirectory and press the plus key.

If the nested subdirectories are currently displayed, the icon of the parent subdirectory contains a minus sign (–). To close the subdirectory, pick the icon containing the minus sign. If you are using the keyboard, highlight the subdirectory and press the minus key.

THE FILE DISPLAY

The files in the currently active subdirectory are displayed in the *file display window*. A small icon appears to the left of each file name. If the file is an executable program, the icon appears as a small rectangle with a horizontal line near the top. If the file is a data file, the icon appears as a sheet of paper with the top right corner folded over.

You may launch an application program by double-clicking on it, or if using the keyboard, by highlighting it and pressing Enter.

Data files may be selected singly or in groups for any file-management operation such as copying, moving, deleting, and so forth. Use the procedure outlined in the section "Highlighting and Selecting Items" to select a single file. If you are using the keyboard, moving the pointer to a file name automatically selects it.

If you want to select a group of files, select the first file, then move the pointer to the next desired file. Hold down the Control key on the keyboard and select the next file. Continue to select files while holding down the Control key, until all desired files are highlighted. This method requires a mouse.

If you are using the keyboard only, you may select a series of files by holding down both the shift key and the spacebar, and moving the pointer with the up or down arrow key.

If you want to include all the files in a subdirectory, select Select all from the Files pull-down menu, or if using the keyboard, hold down the Control key and press the forward-slash (/) key.

If you want to deselect the chosen files, select another file. If you want to deselect files without selecting another, select Deselect all from the File pull-down menu, or if using the keyboard, hold down the Control key and press the backslash (\) key.

When you have selected the desired data files, pick the appropriate DOS file-management command from one of the pull-down menus.

THE PROGRAM WINDOW

The *program window* lists available application software commands, called *program items,* or the names of other nested groups of program items, called *program groups.* In the shell's graphics display, program items appear with a small rectangular icon to the left of the name. Program groups have a similar icon that contains a small window symbol.

The standard version of the DOS shell includes two program items, the Microsoft QuickBASIC programming environment, and the DOS text editor. A discussion of the QuickBASIC programming language is beyond the scope of this book.

The standard version of the DOS shell contains one program group, which is called Disk Utilities. This group contains a short list of program items that handle fundamental file-management tasks: backing up files, restoring files from backup, formatting and copying disks, and undeleting files.

You may configure the program window for other application software.

THE ACTIVE LIST WINDOW

The *active list window* is displayed if you have enabled the *Task Swapper*, a DOS shell feature that allows you to have several applications open at the same time. Each open application is listed in this window, and you may move from application to application by picking the application file name from the window. For more details regarding multiple open applications, refer to the Enable Task Swapper command entry later in Part 3.

DIALOG BOXES

When you invoke certain commands in the DOS Shell, a *dialog box* will appear. An example of a dialog box appears in Figure 3.2. Dialog boxes contain prompts for different parameters associated with the shell command. For example, a dialog box may contain

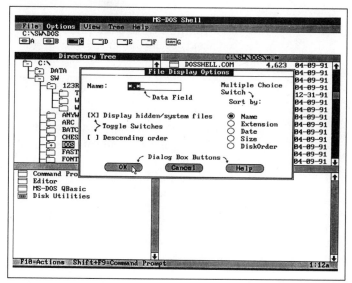

Figure 3.2: A dialog box

one or more *labels*, each followed by a *data field*. You can move between data fields by selecting them or using the keyboard arrow keys or Tab key. Type the appropriate command parameters in the data fields as indicated by the label.

Certain dialog box options are represented by a *toggle switch*, in cases where a command option may be either active or inactive. A toggle switch appears in a dialog box as a label preceded by a pair of brackets ([]). When you select the brackets, an "X" either appears or disappears, indicating that the option is either active or inactive. DOS saves the current state of all toggle switches and presents them as the default the next time the dialog box appears.

If you are to choose one option from among several possibilities, the dialog box will display a *multiple choice list*. This list appears as a column of labels with a small circle to the left of each. Choose one option by selecting the circle. The selected circle is filled, indicating that the option was chosen. You may pick only one option from the list; picking one automatically clears all the others.

Most dialog boxes contain other command switches called *buttons*. Standard dialog box buttons are as follows:

OK	Accepts the chosen dialog box parameters are correct, and either executes the command or causes another dialog box to appear
BACK	Backs up, one at a time, through a series of nested dialog boxes
CLOSE	Closes the current window and returns to the shell without taking any other action
CANCEL	Cancels the command and returns to the shell
HELP	Temporarily suspends the command and displays a window of information regarding the current command
ADVANCED...	Displays a second dialog box of additional parameters that are used in special circumstances

SCROLL BARS

When a dialog box or window contains text or a data list that is too large to fit, a *scroll bar* will appear to the right of the display. Scroll bars are illustrated in Figure 3.1, just to the right of the Directory Tree window and the File Display window. A scroll bar looks like a vertical bar with an arrow at the top and bottom and a small rectangle inside. You can use the scroll bar to scroll the display within a window or dialog box by one of several means:

- *Pick an Arrow with the Pointer.* Selecting the top arrow will scroll the display up, the lower arrow will scroll it down. If you select the arrow and hold the pick button down, the display will scroll continuously.

- *Move the Small Rectangle in the Scroll Bar.* Select the rectangle with the pointer and hold the pick button down. As you move the pointer up and down, you move the rectangle within the scroll bar, and the display within the dialog box will scroll up and down, following the movements of the rectangle.

- *Press the PgUp or PgDn Key* to scroll the display one screenful at a time.

- *Press the Up or Down Arrow Key* to scroll the display one line at a time.

FILE MENU COMMANDS

This section describes the commands that appear when you pick the File keyword in the menu bar. These commands help manage files on disk and control the behavior of files within the DOS shell.

ASSOCIATE

Binds a file name to an application name so that the application is launched when the file name is picked.

● **PROCEDURE** To associate a data file name with an application, first highlight the file name, then select the Associate command. A dialog box appears with the following label:

(extension) files are associated with:

where *extension* is the file extension of the selected file. Enter the line command that will launch the application, then select the OK button or press Enter.

If you have selected more than one data file, a dialog box will be displayed for each unique file extension in your selected files.

If you want to associate several data file types with applications, highlight the application file name (or names) and select the Associate command. A dialog box appears, indicating each highlighted application file in turn. Enter the extensions of the data files to be associated with the indicated application. If you want to include data files without an extension, use a period. When all extensions are entered, pick the OK button.

After you have made an association, you may double-click on any data file with the specified extension, and the associated application will be launched, using the selected file as the default file. DOS accomplishes this by the simple expedient of writing a batch file on the fly, invoking the application with the selected file on the command line.

You cannot associate the same file extension with more than one application. However, up to 20 different file extensions may be associated with the same application.

CHANGE ATTRIBUTES

Permits you to change the attributes of files.

● **PROCEDURE** To change file attributes, first highlight the names of the files whose attributes you intend to change, then select the Change Attributes command. If you have highlighted more than one file, a dialog box appears, offering you the choice of changing attributes one file at a time, or for all selected files. If you choose to change attributes one file at a time, a dialog box appears for each selected file, indicating which attributes are currently set.

An attribute is set when a small arrowhead appears to the left of the attribute name. If you choose to change the attributes for all the files at once, a similar dialog box appears without specifying any file name.

To set an attribute, select the attribute name; the arrowhead will appear. To reverse the effect, select the name a second time; the arrowhead disappears, indicating that the attribute is not set.

The following attributes may be set:

Hidden   Set this attribute to cause DOS not to display the file in directory listings, and to ignore the file when making copies. These files may still appear in the shell if you configure the display to include them. Refer to the section entitled "File Display Options" for details.

System   Set this attribute to cause DOS to see this file as an operating system file. System files behave like hidden files. The only reason a user has to change this attribute is to create two categories of hidden files, perhaps for security purposes.

Read-Only   Set this attribute to prevent any attempt to erase or modify the contents of the file. This is useful in the case of executable files or files that must not be deleted or changed. A few executable files are changed during processing, however; be careful when setting this attribute.

Archive   Set this attribute to indicate that a backup copy of the file exists. The DOS commands XCOPY, BACKUP, and RESTORE honor this setting if the appropriate command line switches are included. Refer to the entries for these commands in Part 2 for details. This attribute is normally turned off after a file has been modified.

COPY

Copies selected files to a new location.

● **PROCEDURE**   If you would like to copy files from one drive to another, first select Dual file lists from the View pull-down menu, and select the appropriate drive letter for each list so that both drives are displayed by the shell, then use one of the techniques outlined below.

Begin the copy process by selecting the files you intend to copy using the standard file selection methods outlined earlier in this chapter.

If you are using the mouse, hold the mouse's pick button down and move the pointer to the destination subdirectory in the directory tree window. If you are copying between subdirectories on the same drive, hold the keyboard's Control key down as well. If you are copying files between drives, it is not necessary to hold the Control key down.

As long as some of the selected files can be successfully copied, the pointer arrow will be replaced by an icon, or in text display mode, a dot. If none of the selected files can be successfully copied (for example, if you have chosen an invalid destination, such as the files' current subdirectory location), the pointer arrow will be replaced by a small circle with a diagonal line running through it. When you have highlighted the desired location, release the Control key if necessary, then release the mouse's pick button, and the files will be copied. You may see a dialog box asking you to confirm the operation.

If you are using the keyboard to copy files, select the files, then pick the Copy command from the File pull-down menu, or press F8. A dialog box appears, displaying the name of each selected file, followed by a data field indicating the location of the copy. The current location of the file is shown as a default. To enter a new location, press the Backspace key (which will blank the data field) or type it in. Alternatively, you may edit the displayed subdirectory path by pressing the left arrow key, which moves the cursor back through the field. Insert new characters by typing them, or delete characters at the cursor position by pressing the Delete key. After you have entered the new subdirectory location, press Enter or select the OK button.

If some of the selected files cannot be moved for any reason, a dialog box appears with an error message. You may cancel the entire operation, or skip the problem file and continue with the remaining files.

If a program window is active, you can use the Copy command to place a copy of a program item in a new program window. First highlight the program item to be copied, then select the Copy command. The F8 function key will not work in this case. After you select the Copy command, open the new window where you would like the copy to reside. Finally, press F2, and the copy appears in the window.

You can copy program items only if the Task Swapper is enabled. Refer to the section entitled "Enable Task Swapper" in Part 3 for details.

CREATE

Adds new subdirectories below the current subdirectory.

● **PROCEDURE** To add a new subdirectory, highlight the name of the parent subdirectory, then select the Create command. A dialog box appears, prompting you to enter the new subdirectory name; enter the name and select the OK button or press Enter. The new subdirectory will be nested below the highlighted one.

DELETE

Removes selected files from the disk.

● **PROCEDURE** To delete files, highlight the names of the files you intend to delete using any of the standard file selection methods outlined earlier, then select the Delete command or press the Delete key on the keyboard. A dialog box appears, displaying the name of each selected file, asking you to confirm the deletion by picking the OK button or pressing Enter. If any of the selected files cannot be deleted, a dialog box appears with a message indicating the nature of the problem; for example, the file has a read-only attribute. You may cancel the entire operation, or skip the problem file and continue with the remaining files.

If a program window is active, you can use the Delete command to delete a program item in the current program window. First highlight the program item to be deleted, then select the Delete command or press the Delete key. A dialog box will appear asking you to confirm the deletion by selecting the OK button or pressing Enter.

You can delete program items only if the Task Swapper is enabled. For details, refer to the section entitled "Enable Task Swapper" further ahead in this part.

DESELECT ALL

Deselects all the files in the currently logged subdirectory.

● **PROCEDURE**   The Deselect All command is a shortcut method for deselecting all the selected files in a subdirectory. It is not available unless at least one file has been selected. If files have been selected in multiple directories, they will all be deselected with this command. To Deselect files, pick this command or hold down the Control key and press the backslash (\) key. The highlighting will be removed from all the files in the file name window.

EXIT

Leaves the DOS shell and returns to the command prompt.

● **PROCEDURE**   To exit the DOS shell, select the Exit command or press Alt-F4. You are returned to the DOS prompt.

MOVE

Changes the subdirectory location of specified files.

● **PROCEDURE**   If you would like to move files from one drive to another, first select "Dual file lists" from the View pull-down menu, and select the appropriate drive letter for each list so that both drives are displayed by the shell.

Begin by selecting the files you intend to move using the standard file selection methods outlined earlier in Part 3.

If you are using the mouse, hold the mouse's pick button down and move the pointer to the desired location. If you are moving files between drives, hold the keyboard's Alt key down as well. If you are moving files between subdirectories on the same drive, it is not necessary to hold the Alt key down.

As long as some of the selected files can be successfully relocated, the pointer arrow will be replaced by the files' icon. If none of the selected files can be successfully relocated (for example, if you have chosen an invalid destination, such as another file name), the pointer arrow will be replaced by a small circle with a diagonal line running through it.

When you have highlighted the desired location, release the Alt key if necessary, then release the mouse pick button, and the files will be moved. You may see a dialog box asking you to confirm the operation.

If you are using the keyboard to move files, select the files, then select the Move command from the File pull-down menu, or press the F7 function key. A dialog box appears, displaying the name of the selected file, followed by a data field indicating its new location. The current location is shown as a default. To enter a new location, press the Backspace key (which will make blank the data field) or type it in. Alternatively, you may edit the displayed subdirectory path by pressing the left arrow key, which moves the cursor back through the field. Insert new characters by typing them, or delete characters at the cursor position by pressing the Delete key. After you have entered the new subdirectory location, press Enter or select the OK button.

If some of the selected files cannot be moved for any reason, a dialog box appears with an error message. You may cancel the entire operation, or skip the problem file and continue with the remaining files.

NEW

Adds a program item to the current program group, or nests a new program group window below the current one.

● **PROCEDURE** The New command only appears when the program window is active. When you select this command, a dialog box appears offering you a choice between a program group or program item. A program group is an additional program window that will be nested below the current program window. A program item is an application that will appear in the currently active program window. After you select one or the other and select the OK button, additional dialog boxes will appear, depending on your selection.

If you choose to create a program group, a dialog box appears with the following prompts:

Title	Enter a title for the program group as you would like it to appear in the program window. The title can be no more than 74 characters.
Help Text	Enter the heading in the DOSSHELL.HLP file that contains help information for this program group. Refer to the section of Part 3 entitled "Customizing the Help File" for details on how to add individual custom help messages.
Password	Enter a password to restrict access to this program group. If you enter a password here, you must reenter it to open the program window or change any of its properties. Passwords are case-sensitive, and must be entered exactly as specified in this data field.

If you choose to create a program item, a dialog box appears with the following prompts:

Program Title	Enter a description of the program as you would like it to appear in the program window. This can be as simple as the program name itself, or a more detailed description up to a limit of 23 characters.
Commands	Enter the DOS line command that will be invoked when this item is picked.

Startup Directory	Enter the name of a subdirectory that will be currently logged at the start of the application.
Application Shortcut Key	Press a special key combination that can be used by the Task Swapper to switch directly to this application when multiple applications are active. This key combination is the equivalent of picking the program from the Active Task List window. Shortcut keys can be any keyboard key pressed while holding down either the Shift key, Control key, or Alt key, provided that they do not conflict with any of the current application's command keys. For example, to switch to the program by pressing Shift-F1, move the cursor to this data box, hold down the Shift key and press the F1 function key. The phrase "SHIFT-F1" will appear in the data box.
Pause After Exit	Activate this toggle switch if you would like DOS to display a "Press any key to continue" prompt upon leaving the application, but before returning to the shell. Deactivate this toggle switch if you would like to return to the shell immediately.
Password	Enter a password to restrict all access to this application. If you enter a password here, you must reenter it to launch the application or change any of the program properties at a later time. Passwords are case-sensitive, and must be entered exactly as specified in this data field.

If you select the "Advanced" button, a dialog box appears with the following prompts:

Help Text	Enter the heading in the DOSSHELL.HLP file that contains help information for this application. Refer to the section of Part 3 entitled "Customizing the Help File" for details on how to add individual custom help messages.

Conventional
Requirement

Enter the minimum amount of memory required by this application. If this field is left blank, all available memory will be used. Data in this field insures that sufficient memory is available before invoking the application. This information may be necessary if you intend to open several applications at once.

XMS Memory

Enter the minimum amount and upper limit of extended memory to be allocated for this application. These fields serve the same purpose as the previous field for applications that require a specific amount of extended memory to run.

Video Mode

You may pick either the Graphics or Text mode switches for programs that require a special video mode not used by the DOS shell. For example, select Graphics if your program requires graphics mode and you are running the shell in text mode.

Reserve
Shortcut Keys

Select these toggle switches to indicate which key combinations may not be used by the shell to switch between this and other applications. If an "X" appears in the toggle box, the key combination is not available to the shell while this program is active. You should disable these if your application requires these special key combinations. If none are selected, you may use any of them to return to the shell while the program remains active. Be certain that the Task Swapper is enabled before attempting to switch between applications.

Prevent
Program
Switch

Select this toggle switch to disable program switching for this application. You should disable switching if attempting to keep this application open will cause conflicts with other applications.

OPEN

Opens highlighted files, program groups, or program items.

● PROCEDURE   The effects of the Open command vary depending on whether a file name, application name, program group, or program item is highlighted.

If a file name is highlighted, the Open command will start an application that has been associated with the file name. Refer to the Associate command entry for details.

If an application name is highlighted, the Open command will launch the application.

If a program group is highlighted, the Open command will activate it and display its contents in the program window area.

If a program item is highlighted, the Open command will invoke its associated command.

PRINT

Sends the contents of a data file to the printer.

● PROCEDURE   The Print command is available only if you have initialized the DOS printing queue before entering the shell. Refer to the PRINT command in Part 2 for details on initializing the printing queue. To use the Print command in the shell, highlight a data file you wish to print, and select the Print command. You may highlight multiple files to print, up to the limit specified when you initialized the printing queue. The default number of files in the queue is 10.

PROPERTIES

Modifies the configuration of program groups and windows.

● PROCEDURE   To reconfigure a program item or group, highlight it and select the Properties command. If the program item or group is password protected, you must enter the password to modify the configuration. A dialog box appears showing the current settings for the program item or group. For details regarding each one of the various settings, refer to the New command entry. After making the appropriate changes to the settings, select the OK button or press Enter.

RENAME

Changes the names of files or subdirectories.

● **PROCEDURE** To rename files or subdirectories, first highlight the files or subdirectories that you want to rename, then select the Rename command. A dialog box appears, indicating the current name of each file, followed by a data field prompting you for the new file name. Enter the new name in the data field, and select the OK button or press Enter.

REORDER

Changes the order of display of program groups and items in the program window.

● **PROCEDURE** To change the location of a program group or item, highlight it and select the Reorder command, then highlight the program group or item that you would like to follow it in the display. Finally, press Enter to move the icon to its new location.

Only one program group or item can be moved at a time. You must highlight the icon to move and select the Reorder command separately for each movement within the display.

RUN

Runs a DOS line command from a dialog box.

● **PROCEDURE** The Run command displays a dialog box containing a single data field. Enter a DOS line command in the data field and pick the OK button to execute the command. You can execute DOS commands or start application software using the Run command.

SEARCH

Looks for files on the currently logged drive.

● **PROCEDURE** When you pick the Search command, a dialog box appears prompting you to enter a *search specification*, a file name or names for which to search. Wildcard characters are allowed, if you would like to search for a group of related files. The dialog box also contains a toggle switch prompting you to search the entire disk. If you disable this toggle, only the currently highlighted subdirectory is searched. Otherwise, the entire disk is searched.

If the search is successful, DOS displays all the file names that matched the search specification. If the search is not successful, DOS displays a message indicating that no matching file names were found.

You may highlight found file names, run them if they are application files, or perform basic file management tasks with them such as copying, renaming, deleting, and so forth.

To return to the shell, press Esc.

SELECT ALL

Selects all the files in the currently logged subdirectory.

● **PROCEDURE** The Select All command is a shortcut method for selecting all the displayed files in a subdirectory. First select the name of a subdirectory to make it current, select the file display window, then select the Select All command or hold down the Control key and press the forward-slash (/) key. All the files in the file name window will be highlighted.

Files that are not actually displayed are ignored by this command.

VIEW FILE CONTENTS

Displays the contents of data files.

● **PROCEDURE** To view the contents of a data file, highlight it and select the View command, or press F9. The contents of the file are displayed on the screen. If the file is too large to be displayed on a single screen, you may scroll through the file using the arrow keys, or the PgUp and PgDn keys. If you are using a mouse with the shell in graphics mode, you may scroll the display by clicking on the key and arrow symbols at the top of the display.

A separate menu bar appears while the file is displayed. Pick the Display keyword to activate a pull-down menu that allows you to display the file in ASCII or hexadecimal formats. Alternatively, you may switch between formats by pressing F9. Pick the View keyword to activate a pull-down menu that offers you two choices: You can select "Repaint the Screen", in case scrolling the file display does not update your screen properly (you can also accomplish this by pressing Shift-F5); or you can select "Restore View," which returns you to the original shell display (you can also accomplish this by pressing ESC). The Help keyword activates the standard Help pull-down menu that is described later on.

You cannot modify files that are displayed using this command. The View command is intended for use on files that only contain ASCII characters, for example, batch files. Executable files or files created using word processors can be displayed, but they may include nonreadable characters that render the display meaningless.

OPTIONS MENU COMMANDS

This section describes the commands that appear when you select the Options keyword in the menu bar. These commands configure certain fundamental aspects of the shell's screen display and control how files are displayed and selected in the File Display window.

COLORS

Controls the color configuration of the shell display.

● **PROCEDURE**   When you select this command, DOS displays a dialog box containing various optional color combinations, depending on the capabilities of your display. If you have a color monitor, these options can range from the jarring "Hot Pink" to the more sedate "Ocean" (the default on color monitors). To choose a color combination, select its name from the dialog box. To preview the appearance of your selected option without exiting the dialog box, select the Preview button. If your chosen color combination is acceptable, select the OK button or press Enter.

If you are a sophisticated user, it is possible for you to create or change the shell's standard color options by editing the DOS-SHELL.INI file with a text editor. If you attempt to do so, first make a backup copy of the original file and save it in a secure location, in case you have problems editing and need to restore the original later.

You may also wish to print out this file and to compare its contents to the appearance of the shell on your screen, to determine how best to modify it to suit your system's display adapter. Look for the section in this file labeled "color=". Within this section you will find several subsections labeled "selection=". These subsections correspond to the shell's standard color schemes and assign colors to various elements within the shell.

CONFIRMATION

Controls the display of confirmation prompts before deleting or overwriting files.

● **PROCEDURE**   When you pick this command, DOS displays a dialog box with three toggle switches. A switch is enabled when an "X" appears in the brackets to the left of the label, and it is disabled if there is only a space between the brackets. All switches are enabled by default. You can use these switches to enable or disable confirmation prompts in three types of operations:

Confirm
on Delete

Enable this switch to display a dialog box asking you to confirm the deletion of each selected file before it is actually erased.

Confirm
on Replace

Enable this switch to display a dialog box asking you for confirmation whenever a file is about to be overwritten; for example, when copying a file from the hard disk to a floppy disk containing a file with the same name.

Confirm
on Mouse
Operation

Enable this switch to display a dialog box asking you for confirmation whenever a mouse operation is about to cause a file to be deleted or overwritten; for example, when moving a file from one subdirectory to another containing a file of the same name.

DISPLAY

Controls the shell resolution and icon display.

● **PROCEDURE**   When you pick this command, DOS displays a dialog box containing several display options, depending on the capabilities of your system.

Simply put, the Display command allows you to choose between *text mode,* which displays only ASCII characters and does not include icons, and *graphics mode,* which permits various graphic character display, including icons. If your system is not capable of graphics display, you cannot select graphics mode options; use text mode instead.

In addition to choosing the mode, you can choose the *resolution* of the shell display. Resolution in this context means the number of lines that the shell is capable of displaying on a single screen; the higher the resolution, the more lines will be displayed. However, at higher resolutions, the text will appear much smaller as well.

To choose a resolution, select one of the displayed options, then select the OK button or press Enter.

ENABLE TASK SWAPPER

Enables multiple programs to remain in RAM, saving you the time it takes to exit and reload them.

● **PROCEDURE** To enable the task swapper, select this command. When task swapping is enabled, a small dot will appear to the left of this menu item, and the Active Task List window will appear.

When task swapping is enabled, you may exit an application by pressing Ctrl-Esc, which returns you to the DOS shell. From the DOS shell, you may launch another application. You may launch as many applications as you have memory in your system to accommodate.

Each application that remains active in memory is added to the list of applications in the Active Task List window.

To add an application to the Active Task List without launching it, highlight the application and press Shift-Enter. To remove an application from the list, simply launch the application and exit it as you normally would using the application's own exit commands instead of Ctrl-Esc.

You can move quickly from one application to the next on the list without returning to the shell. Several different key combinations will allow you to switch from the Shell to any application in the Active Task List, or switch between applications. Table 3.1 outlines these key combinations. In addition, you may define a special shortcut key to bring up any application on the Active Task List. Refer to the New command entry for details on defining shortcut keys.

You cannot disable the Task Swapper or exit the shell while tasks are still active. Close all active applications first by entering them and ending the processing using each application's normal exit routine.

Table 3.1: Task Swapping Key Combinations

KEY COMBINATION	FUNCTION
Ctrl-Esc	Switch to the shell from an application
Alt-Esc	Switch to the next application on the Active Task List
Alt-Shift-Esc	Switch to the previous application on the Active Task List
Alt-Tab	Alternate between two applications

FILE DISPLAY OPTIONS

Controls the included file types and listing order of file names in the File Display window.

● **PROCEDURE** When you select this command, DOS displays a dialog box with the following choices:

Name	Enter the file name specification for the files that are to be included in the File Display window. Wildcard characters are accepted; the default specification is *.*, meaning all file names and extensions.
Display Hidden/ System Files	Enable this toggle switch in order to include the display of files with hidden and system attributes set. If this switch is not enabled, these files are not included. Default is not enabled.

Descending
Order

Enable this toggle to reverse the sorting
order of the files in the display. For
example, if files are sorted
alphabetically and this switch is
enabled, the files will appear in order
from Z to A. Default is not enabled;
alphabetical listings are from A to Z.

You may also select one of the following orders for sorting the file
names:

Name

Alphabetically by file name, then by
extension

Extension

Alphabetically by extension, then by file
name

Date

Chronological order, including time of
creation

Size

Order by file size in bytes

Disk Order

Files displayed in the order they were
created

SELECT ACROSS DIRECTORIES

Controls whether multiple files may be selected in more than one
directory.

● **PROCEDURE**   If you would like to create selection sets of
several files that exist in more than a single subdirectory, activate this
feature by selecting this command. When this feature is activated, a
small dot appears to the left of this command in the menu.

When this feature is not activated, you may create multiple-file
selection sets only within the currently logged subdirectory.

SHOW INFORMATION

Displays a dialog box containing file and disk statistics.

● **PROCEDURE**   To display file statistics, first highlight a file, then pick this command. You may pick this command when multiple files are selected, but information is only shown for the highlighted file. The following information is given:

File
: Indicates the name of the selected file or the last one selected, if you have selected more than one file.

Attributes
: Indicates what attributes are currently set. An "r" indicates that the file is read-only; it cannot be erased or modified. An "h" indicates that the file is classified as a hidden file; it is not normally displayed in directory listings. An "s" indicates that the file is a system file; it is normally suppressed in directory displays, and ignored by the BACKUP and RESTORE commands. An "a" indicates that the archive bit is set; the BACKUP, RESTORE, and XCOPY commands honor the archive bit if the appropriate command-line switches are included at invocation. Refer to the entries for these commands in Part 2 for details.

Number
: Shows the number of files on each drive that are included in the current file selection set.

Size
: Shows the size in bytes of the current selection set.

Directory
: Displays the name of the subdirectory location of the file, the size of the directory, and the number of files therein.

Disk
: Displays the disk drive name (the volume label) of the drive location of the highlighted file, the size of the disk drive, the amount of available space, the number of files, and the number of directories on the drive.

VIEW MENU COMMANDS

This section describes the commands that appear when you select the View keyword in the menu bar. These commands help manage the configuration of the shell's various windows. To change the display, simply select one of the menu options discussed in this section.

ALL FILES

All Files displays the File Display window only, with file, directory, and drive information for the currently highlighted file on the left. This option does not display the Directory Tree, Program, or Active Task List windows. Task swapping is permitted using file names to launch applications and shortcut keys to move between them.

DUAL FILE LISTS

This option functions the same as Single File List, but displays two sets of Drive Display, Directory Tree, and File Display windows, one set above the other. This configuration is useful for more sophisticated file management tasks, and for using the mouse to move and copy files between drives.

PROGRAM LIST

Displays only the Program window, plus the Active Task List window when the Task Swapping feature is enabled. This configuration is good when you are using the shell strictly as an application manager, not as a file manager.

PROGRAM/FILE LIST

This option displays all windows: Directory Tree, File Display, Program, and Active Task List (when the Task Swapping feature is enabled). Allows you to launch applications by selecting program items and file names from the Active Task List. This configuration is the default.

REFRESH

Refresh rereads the current drive's subdirectory and file structure. This may become necessary from time to time because applications (as well as DOS file management commands that are invoked from the DOS prompt within the shell) operate within a secondary command processor. Thus, they have no effect on the shell's current file or directory display windows. If these applications or commands add or delete files or subdirectories, the changes may not be reflected in the display windows when you return to the shell. Invoke this command (or press F5) to make the file and directory displays current.

REPAINT SCREEN

Repaint Screen redraws the shell window display if the display has been marred or otherwise altered by DOS commands, dialog boxes, or applications. Alternatively, you can repaint the screen by pressing Shift-F5.

SINGLE FILE LIST

This option displays the Drive Letter Display, the Directory Tree Window, and the File Display window, but does not display the Program window or the Active Task List window. When the Task Swapper is enabled, you may launch multiple applications by clicking on application file names or data file names associated with applications, and switching between them using shortcut keys. For details on multiple applications, refer to the New command entry in the section entitled "File Menu Commands."

This configuration is more useful when you are using the shell almost exclusively as a file manager, not a program manager.

TREE MENU COMMANDS

This section describes the commands that appear when you select the Tree keyword in the menu bar. These commands change the display of the Directory tree, and are available only when the Directory Tree window is active. To change the directory display, simply pick one of the menu options discussed in this section.

COLLAPSE BRANCH

This option hides the display of subdirectories nested below the highlighted subdirectory. You can achieve the same result by selecting the file folder icon, if it contains a minus sign (–), or by pressing the minus key from the keyboard.

EXPAND ALL

Expand All reveals the entire subdirectory structure of the currently logged drive. The same result occurs if you press Ctrl-* (control-asterisk) from the keyboard.

EXPAND BRANCH

This option reveals all subdirectories, if any, nested below the highlighted subdirectory. You can achieve the same effect by pressing the asterisk (*) key on the keyboard.

EXPAND ONE LEVEL

Expand One Level reveals subdirectories, if any, nested just below the highlighted subdirectory. You can achieve the same effect by selecting the file folder icon, if it contains a plus sign (+), or by pressing the plus key on the keyboard.

HELP MENU COMMANDS

When you select the Help keyword from the menu bar, you are given several categories of available help. When you pick one of the categories, a *help dialog box* appears on the screen. You can scroll through the information in this dialog box using the scroll bar, or you can double-click on any related topic to reveal another dialog box of information. Related topics are easily identifiable, as they are displayed in a highlighted or otherwise contrasting color. You can continue to display as many help windows as you need in order to receive the information you are looking for.

The Help command is extremely flexible, and allows you to navigate throughout the various topics in a free-form way. Each help dialog box has a set of buttons that allow you to jump to commonly used areas:

CLOSE   Returns to the shell

BACK   Backs up through the previously displayed help
        dialog boxes, one at a time

KEYS   Displays topics related to the use of the keyboard

INDEX   Redisplays the Help Index

HELP   Displays information on using the Help feature

The DOS shell also provides context-sensitive help. You can access this help at any time while in the shell, by pressing F1.

You can access Help for various topics using the pull-down menu options discussed in this section.

ABOUT SHELL

This option displays the DOS shell version number and copyright notice.

COMMANDS

This option displays the shell's menu commands, listed in the same order that they appear on the screen, and arranged by menu bar keyword. To get help with a command, scroll through the list and double-click on the command of your choice.

INDEX

This option displays the Help Index, which covers general information about the DOS shell. The Help Index is similar in structure to the Help pull-down menu, and is arranged as follows:

Keyboard   Lists topics that apply to running the shell using the keyboard.

Commands   Lists the shell's menu commands in the same order as they appear in the pull-down menus.

Procedures   Lists the various activities that can be performed using the DOS shell, such as managing files, running multiple applications, changing the shell's configuration, and so forth.

Shell Basics Describes fundamental techniques for using the DOS shell: windows, file lists, picking items, dialog boxes, and so forth.

Using Help   Lists topics related to using the shell's Help command.

For example, to get help with managing multiple applications, select Help from the menu bar, followed by Index, and scroll through the dialog box until you reach the Commands Help section. Select "Options Menu", and you will find "Enable Task Swapper Command." Double-click on this entry to see a brief description of the Task Swapper command, followed by other topics that present the information in more detail.

A simpler alternative to using the Help Index would be to activate the Options pull-down menu, move to the "Enable Task Swapper" command using the keyboard arrow keys, and when the command is highlighted, press F1.

KEYBOARD

This option displays a selection of topics related to using the keyboard in the shell. Information can be found for movement keys, help keys, program management keys, and file management keys, among others.

PROCEDURES

This option displays topics related to file and program management, as well as configuration, customization, and more basic shell techniques.

SHELL BASICS

Shell Basics displays a selection of topics on the fundamental shell techniques: displaying and picking file names; using dialog boxes; using menus, and so forth.

USING HELP

The Using Help option displays information and related topics on how to access the help feature.

Appendix A

Using Batch Files

A *batch file* is an ASCII text file containing a list of DOS commands. Each line in the batch file contains one DOS command plus any required parameters. In its most fundamental form, a batch file allows you to invoke a long series of DOS commands by entering a short command at the DOS prompt. This can simplify repetitive file management tasks and save you quite a few keystrokes.

Batch files can do more than this, however. Special DOS commands apply to batch files; using them, you can make batch files interactive, intelligent, and capable of performing highly complex file management tasks.

ASCII FILES

Batch files normally contain only those characters that you would create by typing: that is, letters, numbers, and standard punctuation marks. There are only a few exceptions to this rule, so if you are new to writing batch files, do not use non-ASCII control characters or high-order bit characters until you are completely comfortable with the basics.

If you are careful, you can create a batch file using a word processor, but you must be certain that you save the file to disk in ASCII format. Word processors refer to ASCII-format files by many different names, for example: DOS text files, ASCII files, Nondocument files, or unformatted files, among others. Consult the documentation for your word processor or text editor to determine how it creates and saves this kind of file.

If you are in doubt about whether you have saved the batch file correctly, you can display the file at the DOS prompt using the TYPE command. If invalid characters exist, they will appear on the screen as strange hieroglyphs (greek letters, little smiling faces, and other strange symbols). If you find such characters in your batch file, there is a strong possibility that it will fail to run.

CREATING BATCH FILES FROM THE DOS PROMPT

You can create simple batch files from the DOS prompt using the COPY CON command. To do so, enter the following:

COPY CON *filename*.**BAT**

where *filename* is the name of the batch file you want to create. After you enter the command, the cursor will drop down one line and you may enter the commands you wish to include in the batch file. Each command, including any necessary command parameters, must occupy its own line in the file. Press Enter after each entry. The commands you enter will not execute, but the cursor will move to the next line.

Type very carefully! Once you press Enter, you cannot move the cursor back up to correct a previous line. If you make a mistake, your only recourse is to end the process and start over from scratch. For this reason, COPY CON is not recommended for anything but the shortest and simplest batch files.

When you have entered all your batch file commands, press F6 or Ctrl-Z. The following symbol will appear on the screen: ^Z.

When you press Enter, DOS copies your commands into the file, and displays the message "1 file(s) copied."

BATCH FILE NAMES

Batch files can be given any valid DOS file name, but they always have the extension .BAT. When you enter the name of a batch file at the DOS prompt (not including the .BAT extension), DOS opens the file and executes the commands it finds just as if you had typed them yourself at the keyboard.

HOW BATCH FILES WORK

As an example of how batch files can save keystrokes, notice the following two-line command sequence. These commands are typical ones that you might invoke every day:

```
DEL C:\BOOK\*.BAK
BACKUP C:\BOOK\*.* A: /S /F
```

The first command erases all the files with the .BAK extension from the C:\BOOK subdirectory. The second invokes the BACKUP utility to make a backup of all the files in the C:\BOOK subdirectory to drive A, including all subdirectories nested below C:\BOOK, as well as formatting any floppy disks that require it.

If you like, you could create a batch file named FINISH.BAT, which includes similar commands that reference any drive letter or subdirectory path on your system. Once you have created FINISH.BAT, you need only enter FINISH at the DOS prompt and DOS will execute the commands for you, thereby reducing over 40 keystrokes to just 7!

Many of the special batch file commands described in this appendix will improve the performance of even these two simple lines. Most of the examples in this appendix use variations on these two command lines to demonstrate the power of different batch file commands. If you like, you can substitute your system's drive letters and subdirectory names and use these examples to demonstrate batch file programming to yourself.

AUTOEXEC.BAT

DOS makes use of one special batch file named AUTOEXEC.BAT. If this batch file exists on the root directory of the boot drive (drives A or C on most systems), the DOS commands in this file will execute automatically whenever the computer is started up or rebooted. This batch file usually contains special configuration and startup DOS commands, but it may contain any valid DOS command you want.

REPLACEABLE PARAMETERS

Many useful batch files do nothing more than slavishly execute the same series of commands each time they run. This is a perfectly acceptable use of batch files, but it carries a drawback: you must write a new batch file for any variation, no matter how slight, in the parameters of a command.

DOS allows you a greater degree of flexibility by permitting you to include up to 9 parameters on the command line when you invoke the batch file (more if you use the SHIFT command). These command line parameters are referenced in the batch file using the percent sign (%) followed by numbers 1 through 9 (0 is reserved for the batch file name itself).

For example, here is a variation on the FINISH.BAT file used above that includes replaceable parameters:

DEL C:%1*.BAK
BACKUP C:%1*.* A: /S /F %2

Having included %1 in the batch file commands in place of subdirectory names, you may now supply the name of any subdirectory path when you invoke FINISH. For example:

FINISH \BOOK

will invoke the commands using the C:\BOOK subdirectory.

Although use of this technique means that you must enter an additional parameter on the command line, you have gained flexibility for your batch file, as it can be used on any subdirectory path in your system, including nested subdirectories. For example, the following will also work:

FINISHBOOK\CHAPTER3

will erase BAK files and backup all of the remaining files on C:\BOOK\CHAPTER3.

If you did not enter a subdirectory name on the command line, DOS would replace the %1 parameter with nothing, and this would cause the commands in the batch file to reference the root directory.

The location of the replaceable parameters on command lines in the batch file is of critical importance. The %2 parameter used in this example allows you to add an additional optional switch to the BACKUP command. For example, you may want to execute this command more than once, adding additional backups to the existing ones, or you may want to start fresh with a new set of backup floppies. If you do not include a second parameter on the command line, DOS will read the BACKUP command and overwrite the disks currently in drive A. Alternatively, you could enter the following:

FINISH \BOOK\CHAPTER /A

and DOS will add the backups from C:\BOOK\CHAPTER to the backup files currently in drive A, rather than overwriting them.

The percent sign can also be used to retrieve DOS environment variables (those variables initialized using the SET command) within batch files. To retrieve an environment variable, the variable name must be enclosed within a pair of percent signs. For example, the following batch file line, using the ECHO command, will display the setting of the COMSPEC variable:

ECHO %COMSPEC%

Environment variables can be quite useful in batch files. For example, imagine that you are using the PROMPT command to send ANSI.SYS escape codes to the screen, but you want to save and return to the current prompt at any time. To do this, first create a batch file called SAVEP.BAT that saves the PROMPT environment variable to a new variable, using these lines:

ECHO OFF
SET SAVDPRMT=%PROMPT%

In addition, you might want to include the SET command line in AUTOEXEC.BAT to be sure that this variable is always on tap.

Once you've saved a prompt, you can return to it anytime using a batch file called RESTP.BAT, which contains the following lines:

ECHO OFF
PROMPT %SAVDPRMT%

Using SAVEP and RESTP, you can save, change, and restore your prompt setting at will.

If a percent sign is not used in batch files according to the rules for replaceable parameters, DOS interprets it as a literal percent sign, for example:

ECHO Just a percent sign - %, nothing more.

will simply display the message exactly as it is seen here.

Many of the batch file commands in this appendix make use of replaceable parameters. Refer to the Examples section for each command for more demonstrations of their use.

BATCH FILE COMMANDS

The batch file command descriptions in this section enable batch files to make choices, perform repetitive tasks, call subroutines, and operate in various ways on optional parameters.

Suppresses the display of the line on the screen. Available only in versions 3.3+.

• SYNTAX

@DOS command

Command lines that include the @ symbol are processed normally, but are not displayed. This symbol must be the first character in the line.

● **EXAMPLES**

```
@ECHO OFF
DEL C:\BOOK\*.BAK
BACKUP C:\BOOK\*.* A: /S /F
```

suppresses the display of the ECHO OFF command.

● **NOTES**   The @ symbol is related to the ECHO OFF command. While ECHO OFF will prevent the display of all subsequent lines, this symbol prevents the display of only the line in which it appears. For this reason it is most often used with ECHO OFF to prevent that particular command from appearing on the screen.

: (COLON)

Indicates a section label in a batch file for use by the GOTO command.

● **SYNTAX**

:label name

In general, the legal characters for label names are the same as the legal characters for DOS file names, the one exception being that the period (.) is not used. Labels allow DOS to jump to any line in a batch file, using the GOTO command to reference a label, positioned just before the target line. See the GOTO entry for details.

● **EXAMPLES**

```
:START
IF NOT EXIST C:\BOOK\*.* GOTO END
DEL C:\BOOK\*.BAK
BACKUP C:\BOOK\*.* A: /S /F
:END
```

will skip the DEL and BACKUP commands if there are no files on C:\BOOK (or if C:\BOOK doesn't exist) by jumping to the END label.

● **NOTES**   DOS allows you to put as many labels as you like in your batch files, and they may be of any length on a single line. However, only the first 8 characters in a label name are significant. Thus, labels named THIS_LABEL and THIS_LABXX are functionally the same.

When a label is encountered in normal sequential batch processing, it is simply ignored.

DOS does not require that you reference every label that you use. If you have used the ECHO OFF command in your batch file, you can use the colon as a substitute for the REM command; DOS will simply treat the line as a long label rather than a command line, and it will not ECHO the line to the screen.

CALL

Invokes a second batch file from within a currently running batch file, then returns to the original batch file. Available only in DOS versions 3.3+.

● **SYNTAX**

CALL (*drive*:\ *path*\) *batch file*

CALL requires the name of another batch file. The .BAT extension is not required. You may include a drive letter and subdirectory path if not the currently logged one.

● **EXAMPLES**

```
@ECHO OFF
CALL WP
DEL C:\BOOK\*.BAK
BACKUP C:\BOOK\*.* A: /S /F
```

calls WP.BAT, then returns to the batch file and invokes the remaining lines.

● **NOTES**   You may nest a series of called batch files several levels deep. DOS will allow you to CALL a batch file from within itself, or have a file that was called call back the original calling file. However, it is up to you to avoid the possibility of an endless loop by including the proper command lines that will allow the batch process to end at the proper time.

Versions earlier than 3.3 can use the following command to load a secondary command processor and run another batch file:

COMMAND /C (*drive*:*path*\) *batch file*

A batch file called using this syntax must include the DOS command EXIT as the final line in order to return to the parent processor and continue processing the original batch file.

If a batch file is invoked from within another batch file by name only, it will process normally, but will not return execution to the original calling file. This technique can be useful in cases where a batch file is making choices between several other batch files, and you need not return to the original.

ECHO

Suppresses the display of a batch file command line on the screen.

● **SYNTAX**

ECHO (*on*/*off*) (*message*)

The purpose of the ECHO command is twofold:

- To avoid cluttering up the screen with unwanted command displays

- To display custom messages on the screen to the user

If you invoke ECHO ON, DOS will display each subsequent line on the screen as it is executed. If you invoke ECHO OFF, the line display is suppressed. If you invoke ECHO without parameters, DOS displays a message indicating the current echo status.

If you invoke ECHO with any other character string, DOS will display the message on the screen, regardless of whether ECHO has been set ON or OFF.

In DOS versions 3.3+, you can use the ECHO command to skip a line on the display. To do so, use the following line:

ECHO+

which has the effect of displaying a null string.

● EXAMPLES

@ECHO OFF
ECHO Loading word processor...
CALL WP
ECHO Deleting BAK files before data backup...
DEL C:%1*.BAK
BACKUP C:%1*.* A: /S /F

displays the messages "Loading word processor..." and "Deleting BAK files before data backup..." before each command line. The command lines themselves are not echoed to the screen.

● NOTES ECHO may be used to redirect character strings to a disk file or printer. This technique will work in batch files as well as from the DOS prompt. For example:

ECHO ^L > PRN

will send a form-feed to most standard printers, where ^L is Ctrl-L, not the caret (^) followed by L.

ECHO Send this character string to a file > TEST.FIL

will send the indicated string to a file named TEST.FIL.

FOR

Allows DOS to execute a command repeatedly.

● SYNTAX

FOR %%variable IN (dataset) DO command (%%variable)

The FOR command creates a condition called a *loop*, in which a single command is executed on a series of file parameters, until all parameters in the series are exhausted. In the above syntax, *dataset* is the series of parameters, *%%variable* is a symbol to be applied sequentially to each item in the data set, and *command* is the DOS command to execute repeatedly, using each updated value for *%%variable*.

In other words, if this syntax were translated into plain English, it would read: "For each item in the indicated list, invoke the command, until you run out of items."

For simplicity's sake, the *%%variable* name is usually a single letter, such as A or X. Do not use numbers as variable names, as DOS will mistake these for replaceable command line parameters. Variable names are case-sensitive. Do not mix %%A and %%a in the same command line.

The *dataset* parameter is always enclosed within parentheses. If the *dataset* parameter includes file names, wildcard characters can be used; every file that matches the specification will be included in the data set. For example, (*.*) would be a data set containing every file on the currently logged drive and subdirectory.

● EXAMPLES

```
@ECHO OFF
FOR %%X IN (*.BAK *.OLD) DO DEL %%X
FOR %%X IN (*.*) DO IF NOT EXIST A:%%X COPY %%X A:
```

deletes all the files with .BAK and .OLD extensions. Then, it copies each file in the current subdirectory to drive A, if that file doesn't already exist on drive A. In other words, the second FOR loop copies only newly created files, skipping those that were copied previously.

• **NOTES** You can create a loop that moves through a list and executes a command without using the variable. For example:

FOR %%A IN (1 2 3 4 5) DO DIR /W

executes the DIR /W command exactly 5 times.

Although used most often in batch files, you may invoke the FOR command from the DOS prompt. If you do, use only a single percent sign in the variable symbol, rather than two.

GOTO

Redirects batch processing to the line immediately following the specified label.

• **SYNTAX**

GOTO *label*

The GOTO command allows different portions of the batch file to execute selectively. By combining labels, which are strings preceded by a colon, with GOTO commands, you can cause batch files to *branch* (skip over or execute specific lines depending on circumstances defined in other commands), or *loop* (repeat the same set of commands until a particular condition is met). For example, GOTO is often used with the IF command to jump to a specific set of commands when a particular logical condition is true.

• **EXAMPLES**

@ECHO OFF
IF NOT EXIST C:%1*.* GOTO ERROR
DEL C:%1*.BAK
BACKUP C:%1*.* A: /S /F %2
GOTO END
:ERROR
ECHO Directory not found, or empty. Please try again.
:END

uses the IF and GOTO commands to determine if a correct parameter (in this case, a valid subdirectory name, such as \DOS, or other subdirectory on your system) was entered on the command line. If DOS cannot find files in the indicated directory (or the directory doesn't exist), GOTO ERROR causes the batch processing to skip the executable lines and jump to the part of the file that displays the error message. If the parameter was valid, the executable lines are invoked, and the GOTO END command skips the error message and jumps to the end of the batch file.

● **NOTES**   A GOTO command can skip forward or backward in the batch file. Using this command, it is possible to create an *endless loop* (a batch file that repeats without ever creating a condition that enables it to stop):

> **:START**
> **DIR /W**
> **GOTO START**
> **:END**

Under such circumstances, your only recourse is to terminate the batch file by pressing Ctrl-C.

Use the GOTO command carefully; it is wise to avoid complicated batch files that skip hither and yon. For best results, keep batch files straightforward and simple.

IF

Tests to determine if a particular condition is true. If the condition is true, executes a command. Otherwise, ignores the command.

● **SYNTAX**

To test a logical condition:

> **IF (*NOT*) (*condition*) *command***

To test for the existence of a file:

> **IF (*NOT*) EXIST (*file(s)*) *command***

The *condition* parameter takes the form of an *equality test*, which compares two strings on the command line using two equal signs (==). For example:

IF "%1"=="/A"

tests to see if the first parameter on the command line is /A. If it is, the condition is evaluated as true, and the command following the condition is executed. If the parameter is anything other than /A, the condition is false, and the command is ignored.

The strings that are compared in equality tests are case-sensitive. Thus, in the above example, /A would not be equal to /a.

The quotation marks around the strings in the above example are not required for every equality test, but using them is good technique, especially when comparing replaceable parameters with literal values, as seen above. Quotation marks allow you to test if a parameter was not entered; for example:

IF "%1"==""

would be true if no parameter had been entered on the batch file command line. Without the quotation marks (or some extra character on both sides of the equality test) there would be no way to test for a null string. The following syntax has the same effect, but its meaning is less obvious since the exclamation point is less likely to be understood as a null string symbol:

IF %1!==!

The condition parameter can also test for the value of DOS environment variables. For example:

IF %COMSPEC%==C:\COMMAND.COM

returns true if the COMSPEC environment variable is C:\COMMAND.COM. Notice that in this case, quotation marks are not necessary, although they could be added on both sides of the equality test if you like.

The condition parameter can also test for the value of *exit codes* that some DOS external commands (and a few third party programs) store in the ERRORLEVEL environment variable.

When testing the value of the ERRORLEVEL variable, the condition will be true if the value stored in ERRORLEVEL is equal to or less than the value specified in the condition parameter. For example, if the ERRORLEVEL value is 1, both of these conditions would be true:

> **IF ERRORLEVEL==1**
>
> **IF ERRORLEVEL==0**

but this condition would be false:

> **IF ERRORLEVEL==2**

Because of this peculiarity, if you want to test for several possible exit codes, start by testing the largest possible ERRORLEVEL value first, and move sequentially through the values until the lowest possible value is tested.

Finally, the IF command can test for the existence of files on disk, using the EXIST keyword. For example:

> **IF EXIST C:\COMMAND.COM**

would return true on many systems, since COMMAND.COM is often found in the root directory of a system's C drive. File names are not case-sensitive.

The NOT keyword reverses any logical condition evaluated by IF. For example:

> **IF NOT "%1"=="/A"**

returns true if the first parameter on the command line is not /A, or had not been entered. The condition will be false only if the first parameter is /A.

> **IF NOT EXIST C:\COMMAND.COM**

returns true if COMMAND.COM cannot be found on the root directory of drive C. If COMMAND.COM is there, the condition is false.

• EXAMPLES

Listing A.1 demonstrates several uses of the IF command. Line 2 causes processing to jump to the NODIR label if the operator failed to enter any parameters on the command line. Line 3 causes processing to jump to the ERROR label if the operator entered a nonexistent subdirectory path, or if no files were found. Line 4 will delete files with a .BAK extension, if any exist (thereby avoiding the confusing "File not found" message). Lines 6–10 test all possible values of the ERRORLEVEL variable and display an appropriate message in each case. The labels and GOTO commands assure that the batch file always branches to the appropriate executable lines.

```
@ECHO OFF

IF ~"%1~"==~"~" GOTO NODIR

IF NOT EXIST C:%1\*.* GOTO ERROR

IF EXIST C:%1\*.BAK DEL C:%1\*.BAK

BACKUP C:%1\*.* A: /S /F %2

IF ERRORLEVEL==4 ECHO Command aborted because of read/write

errors.

IF ERRORLEVEL==3 ECHO Ctrl-C detected.

IF ERRORLEVEL==2 ECHO WARNING! Some files not copied due to

errors.

IF ERRORLEVEL==1 ECHO No files were found to back up.

IF ERRORLEVEL==0 ECHO Backup completed normally.

GOTO END

:NODIR

ECHO Please specify a subdirectory path.

GOTO END

:ERROR

ECHO Directory not found, or empty. Please try again.

:END
```

Listing A.1: A batch file that demonstrates the use of IF

● **NOTES**   IF commands can be nested on the same line. For example:

IF NOT EXIST *.BAK IF NOT EXIST *.OLD ECHO No BAK/OLD files found

tests for the existence of files with a .BAK extension. If none are found, then it tests for files with an .OLD extension. If none are found, it displays the message "No BAK/OLD files found." If files of either type are found, the message will not be displayed.

Nesting IF commands allows you to create complex logical conditions. However, you must be careful that your logic is entirely consistent. For example:

IF "%1"=="/a" IF "%1"=="/A" ECHO Parameter is either /a or /A.

will never display the message, because these nested IF commands require the first parameter to be both /a and /A at the same time, which is impossible.

PAUSE

Pauses batch file processing and waits for the operator to press a key before continuing.

● **SYNTAX**

PAUSE (*message*)

The PAUSE command is useful when you would like to give the operator a chance to read a long message, or to cancel the batch file before continuing.

When the PAUSE command is invoked, it displays a message similar to the following:

Strike a key when ready...

If the user presses a key, the batch file continues. If the user presses Ctrl-C, DOS will prompt for the user to confirm cancellation before cancelling batch processing.

The *message* parameter may be any character string. However, the *message* parameter will appear on the screen only if ECHO is set on, and will include the PAUSE command itself, followed by the "Strike a key" message. If ECHO is OFF, only the "Strike a key" message appears.

In some DOS versions, you may customize the PAUSE message by preceding PAUSE with the ECHO command, echoing your intended message, then redirecting the PAUSE output to NUL.

• EXAMPLES

Listing A.2 shows a batch file that displays a two-line message indicating what is about to happen, then pauses the routine, allowing the operator to cancel or continue.

• NOTES   Not all versions of DOS allow you to redirect the output of the PAUSE command. Experiment with your version to find out if you can.

```
@ECHO OFF

CLS

ECHO Will delete BAK files in, then back up, the C:\BOOK subdirectory.

ECHO Press a key to continue, or Ctrl-C to cancel the command.

PAUSE > NUL

DEL C:\BOOK\*.BAK

BACKUP C:\BOOK\*.* A: /S /F
```

Listing A.2:   A batch file that includes PAUSE

REM

Indicates that the line is a non-executable string, used to place explanatory remarks within the batch file.

● SYNTAX

REM *string*

The REM command allows you to include remarks in the file that explain what the file is doing. These remarks are helpful to others who read the file, or to yourself if you return to edit the file after a time and need to jog your memory.

Lines that begin with REM will display on the screen only if ECHO is set ON; otherwise, they are ignored by DOS.

● EXAMPLES

Listing A.3 shows a batch file that runs normally, but the included remarks are available to anyone who reads the file using a text editor or the TYPE command.

● **NOTES**   If ECHO is set OFF, you can use labels as substitutes for the REM command. Simply place a colon (:) at the beginning of each line. This can make remarks easier to read if they are many lines long.

```
@ECHO OFF

REM This batch file deletes BAK files, backs up what's left.

REM Requires a path name on the command line,

REM otherwise uses the root directory.

IF EXIST C:%1\*.BAK DEL C:%1\*.BAK

REM If a second parameter is included on the command line,

REM it must be a valid parameter used by the BACKUP command:

BACKUP C:%1\*.* A: /S /F %2
```

Listing A.3: A batch file that includes REM

SHIFT

Shifts the location of command line parameters one position to the left, thereby allowing you to include more than 9 parameters on a command line.

● SYNTAX

SHIFT

The SHIFT command uses no parameters. Each time SHIFT is invoked, the parameters on the batch file command line are moved up one position; thus, the %9 parameter becomes %8, %8 becomes %7, and so forth. The %0 parameter is lost. If you have ten or more parameters on the batch file command line, the extra parameters are shifted as well. Thus, the tenth parameter will become the %9 parameter. Since only parameters %0 through %9 can be referenced within a batch file, SHIFT is the only means by which you may include additional parameters on the command line when invoking a batch file.

● EXAMPLES

Listing A.4 shows a batch file that performs a complex loop that allows you to erase .BAK files and make backups of any number of subdirectories that you include on the command line, up to the limit of 127 characters on the command line.

● **NOTES**   You cannot shift in reverse. Each time you execute the SHIFT command, the %0 parameter is lost. If you want to save the %0 parameter, store it in a DOS environment variable before you execute SHIFT. For example:

SET PARAM0=%0
SHIFT

```
@ECHO OFF

: This batch file allows you to run the same two commands on

: any number of subdirectory paths, by looping and shifting.

: Remember to include a backslash (\) in front of each

: subdirectory name on the batch file's command line.

:START

: START is the label for the top of the loop.

: Branch to ERROR label if current %1 parameter is bad:

IF NOT EXIST C:%1\*.* GOTO ERROR

: Otherwise, process:

ECHO Now processing %1 directory --

DEL C:%1\*.BAK

BACKUP C:%1\*.* A: /S /F /A

:LOOP

: This section shifts the parameters and then tests

: to see if a %1 parameter still exists.

: If so, processing branches to the START label:

SHIFT

IF NOT ~"%1~"==~"~" GOTO START

: If the above command does not execute, then all the parameters

: have been used, so the file branches to the end:

GOTO END

: Processing comes here if a bad subdirectory was entered:

:ERROR

ECHO %1 directory not found, or empty.
```

Listing A.4: A batch file that demonstrates SHIFT

```
ECHO Press Ctrl-C to abort, any other key to skip~EL

: Allows for early cancel:

PAUSE > NUL

GOTO LOOP

: Processing comes here when all parameters are used:

:END

ECHO Processing complete~EL
```

Listing A.4: A batch file that demonstrates SHIFT (continued)

BATCH FILE COMMAND ERROR MESSAGES

The following error messages apply to batch file commands:

Batch file missing

You have either deleted the batch file before it finished processing, or DOS could not find the parent routine after completing a nested subroutine. If necessary, reboot the computer. If the batch file was deleted, recover it from your backup copy. Edit the batch file and all nested subroutines to account for the location of all required files.

FOR cannot be nested

You have attempted to include a FOR command within another FOR command. This is not allowed. Edit the batch file to include only one FOR command per line.

Label not found

You have included a GOTO command to a label that is not included in the batch file. Edit the file and correct the label names.

CONFIG.SYS Commands

The CONFIG.SYS file is an ASCII text file that contains instructions to DOS regarding your system configuration. It resides in the root directory of the default starting drive (drive C on most hard-disk systems, or drive A on most floppy-disk systems), and is read by DOS only once, at startup time.

Because CONFIG.SYS is an ASCII file, you can edit it easily using a text editor or word processor that saves files in ASCII format. However, because CONFIG.SYS is read only at startup time, you must reboot your computer to activate any changes you make in CONFIG.SYS.

Certain peripheral devices and applications require that you include commands in CONFIG.SYS. Other commands are used for such purposes as increasing disk-read buffers and the maximum allowed number of open files, loading peripheral device driver software, and increasing the number of logical drive letters in your system.

CONFIG.SYS commands are described in this appendix. For information regarding the standard device drivers supplied with DOS, refer to Appendix C.

With the advent of more sophisticated hardware systems, the order of commands in the CONFIG.SYS file has become increasingly important. If you are configuring your system to take advantage of memory beyond the normal 640Kb limit, be sure that you place any commands to configure this extra memory at the beginning of the CONFIG.SYS file, before invoking any drivers or other software that utilizes this memory.

BREAK

2.0+

Controls when DOS checks for Ctrl-Break entered by the user.

● SYNTAX

BREAK=(ON)/(OFF)

The Ctrl-Break or Ctrl-C key combinations cancel most DOS commands and some applications as well. Normally, DOS checks to see if the user entered Ctrl-Break or Ctrl-C only during functions that transmit data to and from the processor. BREAK=ON will cause DOS to check for cancellation during any DOS function call. This allows the operating system to cancel processing when commands or applications use very little data input and output.

You should avoid using BREAK=ON if applications have their own uses for Ctrl-C. The default status for BREAK is OFF.

● EXAMPLES

BREAK=ON

allows Ctrl-Break checking during any function.

BUFFERS

2.0+

Sets the number of disk-read buffers.

● SYNTAX

BUFFERS= ## (,*n*) (*/options*)

where ## is the number of buffers to be used by DOS.

A buffer is an area of memory set aside for temporary data storage. Buffers can speed up system performance by reducing the number of times DOS must directly access the disk; however, each buffer takes up 528 bytes of RAM, reducing the amount of memory available for processing. Too many buffers will slow a system down.

Because computer systems vary so wildly, there is no hard and fast rule for determining the optimum number of buffers. If you are using DOS versions 4.0+, DOS sets up the default number of buffers based on the size of your RAM. If you are trying to increase system performance by increasing the number of buffers, you might start with the following list, which relates buffers to the size of your hard disk:

Hard Disk Size (in Mbs)	Suggested Number of Buffers
20–32	20
40–80	30
80–120	40
120+	50

In versions 3.3 and earlier, you may specify a maximum of 99 buffers. In versions 4.0, you can specify up to 10,000 buffers if you use the /X option switch.

● OPTIONS

,*n*   (Versions 4.0) Specifies an additional number of *read-ahead buffers*, which store data just beyond the area of the disk being read, where *n* is the number of read-ahead buffers. DOS can anticipate up to 8 sectors of information on disk, so this number should be set to 8 in most cases. Read-ahead buffers further enhance system speed.

/X   (Versions 4.0) Instructs DOS to place the buffers in expanded memory. Allows increase in the maximum number of buffers (up to 10,000). Requires that you have installed an expanded memory manager.

● EXAMPLES

BUFFERS=30,8

installs 30 buffers and 8 read-ahead buffers.

● **NOTES**   If you are using a disk cache to enhance performance, check your documentation for recommendations regarding buffers. Some disk cache schemes may require that you lower the number of buffers or eliminate the BUFFERS command entirely from CONFIG.SYS.

COUNTRY

3.0+

Installs international character sets.

● SYNTAX

COUNTRY=*country code*(*,code page*) (*drive:\path\file.ext*)

Use the COUNTRY command to start your system with a non–United States keyboard and display character set.

The *country code* is a three-digit number; the number of a country is the international telephone dialing prefix. If this command is not used, the default country code is 001 (the United States).

The *code page* is a three-digit number for each country in the COUNTRY.SYS file. The default code page is 437.

The COUNTRY.SYS file is the default file for country-specific data. This file must be located on the root directory if the *file* parameter is not used. Include the *file* parameter if you are using a file other than COUNTRY.SYS, or if the country-specific data file is not located on the root directory.

Refer to Table 2.1 in Part 2 for a list of country codes and code pages.

● EXAMPLES

COUNTRY=002,863

installs the Canadian character set.

COUNTRY=033,437

installs the French character set.

● ERROR MESSAGES

Error in COUNTRY command

DOS did not recognize the syntax you entered in the CONFIG.SYS file. Check the command parameters, edit the syntax, save the file, and reboot the computer. If you are editing CONFIG.SYS with a word processor, be sure to save the file as an ASCII file.

Invalid country code or code page

You have included a country code that DOS does not recognize. Edit this line using a valid country code number, and reboot.

DEVICE

3.0+

Installs device drivers.

● SYNTAX

DEVICE=*driver file* (*/options*)

Many peripheral devices and some applications require that a special controlling software program, called a *device driver,* be loaded in memory. Use the DEVICE command, as instructed by your peripheral device documentation, to load the software program.

By convention, many device drivers have the file extension .SYS. DOS includes a number of device drivers, each with their own special options; refer to Appendix C for a discussion of these device drivers.

● EXAMPLES

DEVICE=ANSI.SYS

loads the DOS extended keyboard and screen driver in versions 2.0+. Refer to Appendix C for examples of other DOS device driver syntax.

● ERROR MESSAGES

Bad or missing device name

DOS could not find the driver file for the device you are attempting to install. Edit CONFIG.SYS and correct the file name or the subdirectory location, then reboot.

Device error

DOS was unable to initialize the device driver. This message appears when a driver file has become corrupted, or if code page parameters are not valid. Copy a valid version of the driver file and font file from backup or master disks. Check that all code page parameters are correct. After editing CONFIG.SYS, reboot the computer.

Sector size too large

The device driver requires a larger sector size than is available on your system. Delete this driver's initialization line from your CONFIG.SYS file.

● **NOTES** Some peripheral device drivers are contained in executable files that may be invoked from the DOS prompt. Be sure that your documentation specifies how your driver file may be loaded. DOS versions 4.0+ include another CONFIG.SYS command, INSTALL, that permits you to load executable files from within CONFIG.SYS.

DEVICEHIGH

5.0

Installs device drivers in reserved memory, if space is available.

● **SYNTAX**

DEVICEHIGH=SIZE=*nn* (*drive:\path*) *driver file* (*/options*)

If you include this command in CONFIG.SYS, you must have previously loaded the HIMEM.SYS device driver using the DEVICE command, plus an expanded memory manager that supports the Microsoft Extended Memory Specification for Upper Memory Blocks (XMS UMB, for short). An example of such an expanded memory manager would be the EMM386.EXE driver that is supplied with MS-DOS. In addition, you must include the command DOS=UMB before using DEVICEHIGH. Refer to the DOS command in the following section for details. If you have not previously loaded these drivers, this command will function identically to the DEVICE command. Refer to Appendix C for details regarding HIMEM.SYS and EMM386.EXE.

Device driver files are normally loaded into conventional memory (0-640Kb) using the DEVICE command. The DEVICEHIGH command attempts to load the driver file into reserved memory (640-1024Kb), if it can find available space. Otherwise, the driver file is loaded in conventional memory.

The *SIZE=nn* parameter indicates the size of the driver file in memory. This number is expressed in hexadecimal (base 16) format.

All other syntax is identical to the DEVICE command. Refer to Appendix C for various examples of DOS device driver syntax.

● EXAMPLES

DEVICEHIGH=SIZE=A4 C:\DOS\ANSI.SYS

loads the ANSI.SYS driver into reserved memory. A4 is the hexadecimal equivalent of the driver's size in bytes.

● ERROR MESSAGES

DEVICEHIGH error messages are the same as for those in the DEVICE command. Refer to the error message section in the DEVICE command entry.

● NOTES   Although the DEVICEHIGH command will conserve conventional memory, the required EMM386 expanded memory driver will take up about 5Kb of conventional memory. Therefore, this option is only practical if you have more than 5Kb of device drivers to load in reserved memory.

DOS

5.0

Loads the operating system in conventional, extended, or reserved memory.

• SYNTAX

DOS=high/low (,umb)

If you include this command in CONFIG.SYS, you must have previously loaded the HIMEM.SYS device driver using the DEVICE command. Refer to Appendix C for details regarding HIMEM.SYS. The UMB parameter is also required to use the DEVICEHIGH and LOADHIGH commands.

Use the HIGH parameter to load DOS into extended memory. By loading DOS in extended memory (that portion of RAM starting at 1024Kb), you can free a significant amount of system RAM for application software. You must have sufficient extended memory installed in your system to take advantage of this feature.

Use the LOW parameter to load DOS in *conventional memory* (memory between 0Kb and 640Kb). This is the default location for DOS if you do not include this command in CONFIG.SYS.

If you include the optional *UMB* parameter, DOS will attempt to load as much of itself as it can into *reserved memory* (that portion of RAM between 640Kb and 1024Kb). Any remaining part of the operating system will be loaded into memory as indicated by the HIGH or LOW parameter.

However, the UMB parameter is valid only if you have loaded an expanded memory manager that supports the XMS UMB allocation

routines used by DOS; for example, the EMM386.EXE driver supplied with MS-DOS. If you have not previously loaded such a
driver, the UMB parameter has no effect.

● EXAMPLES

DOS=HIGH,UMB

loads DOS into reserved memory, with any remainder placed in extended memory.

DOS=LOW,UMB

loads DOS into reserved memory, with any remainder placed in
conventional memory.

● ERROR MESSAGES

HMA not available

DOS cannot load itself in the high memory area. Check that the line
DEVICE=HIMEM.SYS precedes the line DOS=HIGH in the CON-
FIG.SYS file.

● **NOTES**   This command is available only on 80386 or 80486
machines, and some advanced 80286 machines that are capable of
mapping extended and reserved memory.

FCBS

3.0+

Specifies the number of open files using file control blocks.

● SYNTAX

FCBS=maximum, open

The FCBS command is used primarily with networking schemes that control the number of open files by means of *file control blocks*, which are pointers to the location of open files on disk. Include this command in CONFIG.SYS if you are using a network, the SHARE command, or software that manages open files by this method, if your software documentation instructs you to do so.

The *maximum* parameter indicates the maximum number of open file control blocks, from 1 to 255. Default is 4.

The *open* parameter indicates the number of files that will not automatically close if processing attempts to open more files than allowed by the maximum parameter. If processing attempts to open more files than allowed by the FCBS command, DOS displays an error message.

● EXAMPLES

FCBS=48,8

specifies a maximum of 48 open file control blocks, with up to 8 files protected from automatic closing if processing attempts to open more than 48.

FCBS=1,1

sets the maximum number of file control blocks to 1.

● **NOTES**   DOS versions 2.0+ use a different scheme of *file handles* for controlling the number of concurrently open files. This scheme is controlled by the FILES command. Use the FILES command with DOS versions 2.0+, unless you are instructed to use the FCBS command.

If no other software requires this setting and you are not using a network, you can conserve a little memory by setting FCBS to 1.

FILES

2.0+

Sets the maximum allowed number of simultaneously open files.

● SYNTAX

FILES=*n*

The *n* parameter indicates the maximum number of concurrently open files. Default is 8; maximum number is 255. If you exceed the maximum number of open files during processing, DOS displays the message "Too many files are open."

● EXAMPLES

FILES=25

indicates that a maximum of 25 files may be open at once.

● ERROR MESSAGES

No free file handles

You have exceeded the maximum number of open files on your system. Edit this line to increase the maximum allowable number of open files.

● NOTES Each increment to this parameter decreases the amount of RAM available to applications by 128 bytes; therefore, it serves no purpose to set this parameter any higher than the maximum possible number of files for your application. Refer to your software documentation to determine which one requires the largest number of open files, and set the FILES command to that number.

You can experiment to determine the lowest practical number of open files on your system.

INSTALL

4.0+

Loads terminate-and-stay-resident (TSR) software.

● SYNTAX

INSTALL=(*drive:*\ *path*\ **)***file.ext*

TSR programs are normally loaded by means of executable files at the DOS prompt. The INSTALL command lets you load TSR programs at the earliest point in the power-on process; this can help reduce conflicts by loading such programs in areas of memory where they are least likely to cause RAM addressing conflicts with other applications. Include a drive letter and subdirectory location if the file does not exist on the root directory. The file extension (.COM or .EXE) is required.

Four DOS external commands may be loaded this way: FAST-OPEN.EXE, KEYB.COM, NLSFUNC.EXE, and SHARE.EXE. Refer to Part 2 for details regarding these commands.

● EXAMPLES

INSTALL=C:\ DOS\ SHARE.EXE

installs the SHARE command, from the file located on the C:\DOS subdirectory.

● NOTES   This command speeds installation and minimizes ad-dressing programs, but it will not prevent interrupt conflicts between

TSR programs and applications. Some TSR programs permit you to unload them if they cause conflicts; in other cases, you may have to choose not to install TSR programs that cannot coexist with other software.

LASTDRIVE

3.0+

Specifies the largest logical drive letter to be used by the system.

● SYNTAX

LASTDRIVE=*drive*

The *drive* parameter is a letter from A to Z. The colon is not used in this syntax.

This command alerts DOS that you will be using more logical drive letters than actual logical drives in the system; for example, if you intend to use the SUBST command to assign drive letters to sub-directory names.

● EXAMPLES

LASTDRIVE=H

sets a maximum of 8 logical drive letters.

● **NOTES**   DOS will set the highest drive letter automatically. You only need to use this command if your processing requires additional "dummy" logical drive letters, that is, more than the amount for which your system is configured.

Each additional drive letter over E takes up 81 bytes of RAM. You can save a little memory by setting no more than your actual upper limit of drive letters.

REM

4.0+

Indicates a comment line to be ignored by DOS.

● SYNTAX

REM (*comment*)

The REM command allows you to place comments in CONFIG.SYS for documenting the purposes of commands, or refreshing your memory if you return to edit the file after a long period of time. You can also use the REM command to "comment out" certain CONFIG.SYS commands that you use only occasionally.

● EXAMPLES

REM The following loads the XMS extended memory
REM controller at 1536K
REM DEVICE=C:\DOS\HIMEM.SYS /INT15=1536

The first two lines are a simple comment. On the third line, the REM command blocks loading of the HIMEM.SYS driver.

SHELL

3.0+

Installs an alternate COMMAND.COM file, and changes the environment size.

● SYNTAX

SHELL=(*drive:\path*)COMMAND.COM (*/options*)

DOS looks for COMMAND.COM in the root directory of the drive used to load the operating system (drive C on many hard-disk systems, drive A on floppy-disk systems). Use the SHELL command to indicate a different location for COMMAND.COM; for example, you might put COMMAND.COM on a RAM disk to increase performance speed and reduce disk changes on systems without a hard disk.

If you are using a large number of environment variables in your system and run out of environment space, you can also use the SHELL command to increase its size. The default size of the environment space is 160 bytes; the maximum allowable environment size is 32,768 bytes.

● OPTIONS

/P   Loads the specified COMMAND.COM as the primary processor. Without this parameter, the specified COMMAND.COM is loaded as a secondary processor, and the EXIT command will return to the COMMAND.COM that was initially loaded.

/E:*nnn*   Indicates the size of the environment space. In
            versions 3.2+, *nnn* equals the size of the
            environment space in bytes; for example, 512 to
            indicate 512 bytes. In earlier versions, *nnn* is the
            number of 16-byte chunks of memory used for the
            environment; for example, 32 to indicate 512 bytes.

● EXAMPLES

SHELL=D:COMMAND.COM /E:512 /P

loads the copy of COMMAND.COM on drive D as the primary
processor, and increases the size of the environment to 512 bytes.

● ERROR MESSAGES

Specified COMMAND search directory bad

DOS cannot find the COMMAND.COM file based on the syntax
you have entered for the SHELL command. Edit CONFIG.SYS to
correct this line, and reboot the computer.

STACKS

3.2+

Sets dynamic allocation of stack space.

● SYNTAX

STACKS=frames,size

Dynamic stack space allocation permits multiple interrupt calls to call each other without crashing the system.

The *frames* parameter sets the number of stack frames. Default is 9, except for IBM-PC, XT, or portable machines, where the default is 0. Valid numbers of frames are from 8 to 64. The *size* parameter indicates the size of each frame. Default is 128, except for IBM-PC, XT, or portable machines, where the default is 0. Valid frame sizes are from 32 to 512 bytes.

● EXAMPLES

STACKS=18,128

increases the dynamic stack capacity to 18 frames, 128 bytes each.

STACKS=0,0

turns off dynamic stack allocation.

● ERROR MESSAGES

Internal stack overflow

DOS could not find enough stack space to complete processing. Edit this line to increase the number of stacks and reboot the computer.

Invalid STACK parameter

DOS could not recognize the syntax for this command. Edit CONFIG.SYS to correct the parameters, and reboot the computer.

● NOTES
This command is generally not required, unless your application documentation calls for it. You may conserve memory on systems with tight RAM requirements by setting the STACKS parameters to 0.

SWITCHES

4.0+

Allows backward compatibility from 101-key keyboards, and movement of the WINA20.386 file from the root directory.

• SYNTAX

SWITCHES=(/K or /W)

If older programs cannot recognize some of the keys on your extended, 101-key keyboard, use this command with the /K switch to cause the keyboard to emulate an older style, 84-key keyboard.

If you want to move the WINA20.386 file out of your root directory, use the /W switch with this command.

If you are running WINDOWS version 3.0 on an 80386 computer and want to move the WINA20.386 file out of your root directory, use the /W switch with this command. You must also add the following command to the enhanced section of your Windows' SYSTEM.INI file:

DEVICE=(*drive:\path*) WINA20.386

where *drive:\path* indicates the new location of the WINA20.386 file.

Appendix C

Standard MS-DOS Device Driver Files

MS-DOS version 5.0 includes ten standard device driver files for use in creating optional system configurations. These device drivers control memory allocations, display options, and disk drive usage. Different hardware manufacturers may license their own version of DOS with other device drivers, or drivers with syntax different than that listed here. If you are using another manufacturer's version of DOS, be sure to check their documentation for changes to the syntax described in this appendix.

The drivers in this section are all loaded into memory using the DEVICE command in the CONFIG.SYS file; except where otherwise noted, you may also load these drivers using the DEVICEHIGH command, provided that you have previously loaded HIMEM.SYS and EMM386.SYS.

ANSI.SYS

| 2.0+ |

Extended screen and keyboard device driver.

● SYNTAX

DEVICE=(*drive:* \ *path* \ ) ANSI.SYS (/X)(/ *options*)

This driver loads extended capabilities for adapting the screen display and modifying the keyboard keys, to be used by applications that require these features. Consult your application's documentation to determine if it requires ANSI.SYS.

You may use the functions in ANSI.SYS to modify your screen and keyboard. Table C.1 lists the various ANSI Escape functions available once ANSI.SYS is loaded. Table C.2 lists the graphics mode and color codes. Table C.3 lists screen width codes. Tables C.4–C.7 list the key codes used to redefine keyboard keys. Additional codes might be available for other keyboards.

● OPTIONS

/X   (Versions 4.0+) Enables keyboard
                redefinition features for duplicate keys
                on the newer, 101-key keyboards. This
                option switch does not load ANSI.SYS
                into extended memory. Use the
                DEVICEHIGH command instead.

/K   (Versions 5.0+) Ignores extended keys
                on 101-key keyboards.

Table C.1: ANSI Escape Sequences for Use in Batch Files

FUNCTION	SEQUENCE	PARAMETER
Cursor to fixed position	ESC[*line;column*H	*line* = Cursor line number
		column = Cursor column number
Cursor up	ESC[*lines*A	*lines* = Number of lines up
Cursor down	ESC[*lines*B	*lines* = Number of lines down
Cursor right	ESC[*columns*C	*columns* = Number of columns right
Cursor left	ESC[*columns*D	*columns* = Number of columns left
Display cursor position	ESC[6n	
Save cursor position	ESC[s	
Restore cursor position	ESC[u	
Erase display	ESC[2J	
Erase line from cursor	ESC[K	
Set graphics mode/color	ESC[*code;...;code*m	*code* = Mode/color code(s)
Set screen width	ESC[=*code*h	*code* = Screen width code
Reset screen width	ESC[=*code*l	*code* = Screen width code

Table C.1: ANSI Escape Sequences for Use in Batch Files (cont.)

FUNCTION	SEQUENCE	PARAMETER
Redefine keystroke	ESC[*key;"string"*;p	*key* = Key code, *string* = New keystroke character(s)

Note: The letters ESC stand for the ASCII "Escape" character (Decimal 27; Hex 1B). Your text editor must be capable of producing this character to enter these sequences in your files.

Table C.2: ANSI Graphics Mode and Color Codes

CODE	MEANING
0	Attributes off
1	Bold
2	Underscore (monochrome)
5	Blinking
7	Reverse video
8	Hidden
30	Foreground black
31	Foreground red
32	Foreground green
33	Foreground yellow
34	Foreground blue
35	Foreground magenta
36	Foreground cyan
37	Foreground white
40	Background black
41	Background red

Table C.2: ANSI Graphics Mode and Color Codes (cont.)

CODE	MEANING
42	Background green
43	Background yellow
44	Background blue
45	Background magenta
46	Background cyan
47	Background white

Table C.3: ANSI Screen Width Codes

CODE	MEANING
0	B&W 40x25
1	Color 40x25
2	B&W 80x25
3	Color 80x25
4	Color 320x200
5	B&W 320x200
6	B&W 640x200
7	Word wrap on
13	16-Color 320x200 (graphics)
14	Color 640x200
15	Mono 640x350
16	Color 640x350
17	Mono 640x480
18	Color 640x480
19	256-Color 320x200

Table C.4: ANSI Key Codes—Alphabet Keys

	x	X	CTRL-*X*	ALT-*X*
a	97	65	1	0;30
b	98	66	2	0;48
c	99	67	3	0;46
d	100	68	4	0;32
e	101	69	5	0;18
f	102	70	6	0;33
g	103	71	7	0;34
h	104	72	8	0;35
i	105	73	9	0;23
j	106	74	10	0;36
k	107	75	11	0;37
l	108	76	12	0;38
m	109	77	13	0;50
n	110	78	14	0;49
o	111	79	15	0;24
p	112	80	16	0;25
q	113	81	17	0;16
r	114	82	18	0;19
s	115	83	19	0;31
t	116	84	20	0;20
u	117	85	21	0;22
v	118	86	22	0;47
w	119	87	23	0;17
x	120	88	24	0;45
y	121	89	25	0;21

Table C.4: ANSI Key Codes—Alphabet Keys (cont.)

	x	**X**	**CTRL-*X***	**ALT-*X***
z	122	90	26	0;44

Note: The first column lists the letters of the alphabet; the second column (x) shows the code that corresponds to each lowercase letter; the third column (X) shows the code that corresponds to each uppercase letter; the fourth column (Ctrl-X) shows the code that corresponds to each letter combined with the Control key; and the fifth column (Alt-X) shows the code that corresponds to each letter combined with the Alt key.

Table C.5: ANSI Key Codes—Function Keys

	F*n*	**SHIFT-F*n***	**CTRL-F*n***	**ALT-F*n***
F1	0;59	0;84	0;94	0;104
F2	0;60	0;85	0;95	0;105
F3	0;61	0;86	0;96	0;106
F4	0;62	0;87	0;97	0;107
F5	0;63	0;88	0;98	0;108
F6	0;64	0;89	0;99	0;109
F7	0;65	0;90	0;100	0;110
F8	0;66	0;91	0;101	0;111
F9	0;67	0;92	0;102	0;112
F10	0;68	0;93	0;103	0;113
F11	0;133	0;135	0;137	0;139
F12	0;134	0;136	0;138	0;140

Note: The first column lists the function keys; the second column (Fn) shows the code that corresponds to each function key; the third column (Shift-Fn) shows the code that corresponds to each function key combined with the Shift key; the fourth column (Ctrl-n) shows the code that corresponds to each function key combined with the Control key; and the fifth column (Alt-Fn) shows the code that corresponds to each function key combined with the Alt key.

Table C.6: ANSI Key Codes—Number/Punctuation Keys

	n	SHIFT-*n*	ALT-*n*
0	48	41 ())	0;129
1	49	33 (!)	0;120
2	50	64 (@)	0;121
3	51	35 (#)	0;122
4	52	36 ($)	0;123
5	53	37 (%)	0;124
6	54	94 (^)	0;125
7	55	38 (&)	0;126
8	56	42 (*)	0;127
9	57	40 (()	0;128

Note: The first column lists the number keys; the second column (n) shows the code that corresponds to each number; the third column (Shift-n) shows the code that corresponds to each number combined with the Shift key, as well as the punctuation key associated with each combination; and the fourth column (Alt-n) shows the code that corresponds to each number combined with the Alt key.

Table C.7: ANSI Key Codes—Miscellaneous Keys

	K	SHIFT-*K*	CTRL-*K*	ALT-*K*
Space	32			
-	45	95		0;130
=	61	43		0;131
Tab	9	0;15		
Home	0;71	55	0;119	
↑	0;72	56		
↓	0;80	54		
←	0;75	52	0;115	

Table C.7: ANSI Key Codes—Miscellaneous Keys (cont.)

	K	**SHIFT-K**	**CTRL-K**	**ALT-K**
→	0;77		0;116	
PgUp	0;73	57	0;132	
PgDn	0;81	51	0;118	
End	0;79	49	0;117	
Ins	0;82	48		
Del	0;83	46		
PrtScr			0;114	
Null	0;3			

Note: The first column lists various keys; the second column (K) shows the code that corresponds to each key; the third column (Shift-K) shows the code that corresponds to each key combined with the Shift key; the fourth column (Ctrl-K) shows the code that corresponds to each key combined with the Control key; and the fifth column (Alt-K) shows the code that corresponds to each key combined with the Alt key.

● EXAMPLES

DEVICE=C:\DOS\ANSI.SYS /X

loads the full set of ANSI keyboard and screen redefinition functions.

The following examples show ANSI escape sequences that can be entered by means of batch files once you have loaded the ANSI.SYS driver. When you key in these examples, do not treat the letters ESC literally. They stand for the ASCII "Escape" character (Decimal 27, or hexadecimal 1B), which on some displays will look like a small arrow pointing to the left or a caret followed by a left bracket (^[). Be certain that your text editor can produce this character, and use it in place of the letters ESC.

ECHO ESC(34;46m

sets screen colors to blue letters on a cyan background.

ECHO ESC(2J

clears screen after setting new colors.

ECHO ESC(0;67;"COPY *.* A:"p

ECHO ESC(0;68;"COPY *.* B:"p

redefines the F9 function key to invoke the command **COPY *.* A:**
and the F10 function key to invoke the command **COPY *.* B:**.

● ERROR MESSAGES

Bad or missing ANSI.SYS

DOS cannot locate the ANSI.SYS driver, or the driver has become
corrupted. Copy the ANSI.SYS file from backup onto the root directory, or specify the location of the file on the initialization line in
CONFIG.SYS.

ANSI.SYS must be installed to perform requested function

You have neglected to install ANSI.SYS, or have not used the correct syntax in the CONFIG.SYS file. Check the syntax in CON-
FIG.SYS and reboot the computer.

DISPLAY.SYS

3.3+

Loads international font sets for the screen display.

● SYNTAX

**DEVICE=(*drive:\path*) DISPLAY.SYS CON=(*type* (,*code*
page,additional))**

To specify an international character set using the DISPLAY.SYS driver, indicate a display type as well as at least one character set code page. The *type* parameter is one of the following:

MONO   Monochrome display adapter

CGA   Standard IBM color graphics adapter

EGA   Enhanced graphics adapter, also VGA displays

LCD   PC convertible adapter

For DOS versions 4.0+ use EGA for all displays except the PC convertible.

The *code page* parameter is a three-digit number representing international character sets, as outlined in Table 2.1 in Part 2.

The *additional* parameter is a number indicating how many extra code pages you intend to prepare using the MODE command. Refer to the MODE command entry in Part 2 for details on preparing code pages. Your system must be capable of handling multiple international character sets.

• EXAMPLES

DEVICE=C:\DOS\DISPLAY.SYS CON=(EGA,863,1)

loads the Canadian screen display font set and specifies that one additional font set will be prepared using the MODE command in versions 4.0+. In versions 3.3 and earlier, use 002 as the code page to load the Canadian set.

• ERROR MESSAGES

Code page drive cannot be initialized

You may have included an invalid parameter in the DISPLAY.SYS initialization line. Edit CONFIG.SYS and correct the syntax, then reboot the computer.

Invalid syntax on DISPLAY.SYS code page driver

DOS does not understand the syntax you have entered on the DISPLAY.SYS initialization line in CONFIG.SYS. Edit this line in the

CONFIG.SYS file and reboot the computer. If you are using a word processor to edit the file, be sure to save it in ASCII format.

Required font not loaded

DISPLAY.SYS has not been initialized to include the desired font. Edit CONFIG.SYS, increasing the number of subfonts, and reboot the computer.

● **NOTES**   As an alternative to this driver, the COUNTRY.SYS and KEYBOARD.SYS files are also used to specify code page switching. COUNTRY.SYS is specified as a parameter to the NLSFUNC command; KEYBOARD.SYS is a parameter of the KEYB command that specifies several international keyboard layouts.

DRIVER.SYS

3.2+

Assigns logical drive letters to a physical drive device.

● SYNTAX

DEVICE=(*drive:\path*) DRIVER.SYS (*/options*)

Each time this command is invoked, DOS assigns the next available drive letter to the specified device. The options allow you to specify exact formatting requirements for the new logical drive. You can assign additional drive letters to the same or other devices by repeating this command in CONFIG.SYS.

● OPTIONS

/D:*nnn*   Indicates the drive number, where *nnn* is a number from 0 to 127. 0 refers to the first drive, usually A.

/T:*nnn*   Indicates the number of tracks on each side, where *nnn* is a number from 1 to 999.

/S:*nn*   Indicates the number of sectors per track, where *nn* is a number from 1 to 99.

/H:*nn*   Indicates the number of heads per drive, where *nn* is a number from 1 to 99.

/C   Enables change-line support, a feature that allows DOS to detect if a floppy disk has been changed in the drive during operations. Default is no change-line support.

/F:*n*   Specifies the drive format, where *n* is a number indicating one of the following formats:

> 0 = 5.25", Single- or double-density floppy
>
> 1 = 5.25", High-density (1.2Mb) floppy
>
> 2 = 3.5", 720Kb diskette
>
> 7 = 3.5", 1.44Mb diskette

Default is 2.

• EXAMPLES

DEVICE=C:\DOS\DRIVER.SYS /D:1 /T:80 /S:9 /H:2 /F:2

assigns the next available drive letter to drive B, and indicates that it is to be treated as a 3.5", 720Kb drive. Assuming a system with two floppy drives and a single hard disk, this command would allow drive B to function as both drive B and drive D. Thus, you could copy disks in the same drive by entering the command COPY B:*.* D:, and DOS would prompt you to switch disks as required to make the copy.

DEVICE=C:\DOS\DRIVER.SYS /D:0 /T:80 /S:15 /H:2 /F:1

assigns the next available drive letter to drive A, and indicates that it is to be treated as a high-density (1.2Mb) floppy drive. Given the same assumptions as in the previous example, you could then copy disks in drive A by entering the command COPY A:*.* D:.

● ERROR MESSAGES

No drive specified

You have not included the physical drive number in the initialization line in CONFIG.SYS. Edit the CONFIG.SYS file and reboot the computer.

● NOTES   DRIVER.SYS is intended for use by systems with external disk drive adapters, and for systems that cannot normally copy files from disk to disk on the same floppy-disk drive.

The SUBST command also assigns new logical drive letters to existing drives, and is usually easier to implement and understand.

If you are setting up RAM disks, place the RAM disk commands after the DRIVER.SYS commands.

EGA.SYS

5.0+

Driver for saving and restoring EGA screens used with the DOS Shell Task Swapper.

● SYNTAX

DEVICE=(drive:\path\) EGA.SYS

This driver loads saving and restoring capabilities for EGA screens. Use this driver if your system has trouble handling screen displays when moving between programs in the DOS Shell. There are no options, and its functions are transparent to the user.

● EXAMPLES

DEVICE=C:\DOS\EGA.SYS

loads the EGA screen saver functions, when the EGA.SYS file is stored on the C:\DOS subdirectory.

EMM386.EXE

4.0+

Installs expanded and reserved memory support for 80386 and 80486 computer systems with extended memory.

● SYNTAX

DEVICE=(drive:\path) EMM386.EXE (ON/OFF/AUTO) (size) (/options) (RAM/NOEMS)

The EMM386.SYS expanded-memory manager should be installed only after the HIMEM.SYS (extended-memory manager) is installed. Do not load this driver using the DEVICEHIGH command. The DEVICEHIGH command is valid only after this driver is completely loaded.

● OPTIONS

size
(Version 4.0+) Required only if you intend to configure a portion of your system's total extended memory as expanded memory, where *size* is a number indicating the expanded memory size in kilobytes (e.g., 64 equals 64 Kb). If you leave out this parameter and the NOEMS parameter, up to 256K of extended memory will be used as expanded memory.

AUTO
Loads the Expanded Memory driver, but activates the driver only when a program calls for expanded memory.

A=*nnn*
Specifies the number of alternate register sets to use for multitasking, where *nnn* is the number of sets. The valid range is from 0 through 254. Default is 7.

B=*nnnn*
Specifies the lowest address in RAM to be used as a bank for swapping portions of RAM to and from expanded memory. Valid addresses are from 1000 through 4000 hex. Default is 4000 hex.

D=*nnn*
Specifies the amount of memory to reserve for buffered direct-memory access, where *nnn* is the amount of memory in kilobytes. The valid range is 16–256Kb. Default is 16.

FRAME=*nnnn*
Specifies the address in memory for the expanded-memory page-frame segment base, where *nnnn* is a number that specifies the base address in hexadecimal. Valid addresses are from 8000 through 9000 hex, and C000 through E000 hex, in increments of 400 hex.

H=*nnn*
Specifies the number of segment handles to be used, where *nnn* is the number of handles. The valid range is 2–255 handles. Default is 64.

I=*nnnn–nnnn*	Specifies a range of RAM addresses to be used as page-frame addresses. Valid addresses are from A000 through FFFF hex, and are rounded down to the nearest 4Kb.
L=*nnnn*	Prevents a portion of extended memory from being used as expanded memory, where *nnnn* is the amount of extended memory to exclude.
M*n*	Specifies the address in memory for the expanded-memory page frame, where *n* is a number that specifies the base address according to the following table:

1	= C000	5	= D000	10	= 8000
2	= C400	6	= D400	11	= 8400
3	= C800	7	= D800	12	= 8800
4	= CC00	8	= DC00	13	= 8C00
		9	= E000	14	= 9000

Use numbers 10 through 14 on computers with 512Kb of conventional memory.

NOEMS	Disables all expanded-memory support if you have included the RAM parameter and want reserved-memory support only.
ON	(Version 5.0+) Activates the Expanded Memory driver immediately upon loading. This is the default setting.
OFF	Loads, but does not activate, the Expanded Memory driver.
/P*nnnn*	Specifies the hexadecimal memory address for the page frame, where *nnnn* is a number that specifies the address. Valid addresses are from 8000 through 9000 hex, and C000 through E000 hex, in increments of 400 hex.

P*n=nnnn*	Specifies the page address, where *n* is the page number (0–255), and *nnnn* is the address in memory. Valid addresses are from 8000 through 9C00 hex, and C000 through EC00 hex, in increments of 400 hex.
RAM	Enables support for *reserved memory*, that area of RAM between 640Kb and 1024Kb. If support for this memory is enabled, DOS will find and utilize unused portions of this area for loading other device drivers with the DEVICEHIGH (CONFIG.SYS) and LOADHIGH (command prompt) commands.
W=[ON/OFF]	Enables support for the Weitek math coprocessor if set to ON. Default is OFF.
X=*nnnn–nnnn*	Excludes a range of RAM addresses for use as page-frame addresses. Valid addresses are from A000 through FFFF hex, and are rounded down to the nearest 4Kb. This option takes precedence over the I= option if the two ranges overlap.

● NOTES

The /P*nnnn* option is the only option that requires the use of the forward slash character.

If you use the M, FRAME, or /P options, do not specify the addresses for pages 0–3.

● EXAMPLES

DEVICE=C:\DOS\EMM386.EXE 1024 RAM

enables expanded-memory support for 1Kb of expanded memory, plus reserved-memory support.

DEVICE=C:\DOS\EMM386.EXE RAM NOEMS

enables support for reserved memory only.

HIMEM.SYS

4.0+

Loads extended memory support using Microsoft's XMS extended memory specification.

● SYNTAX

DEVICE=(*drive:**path*) HIMEM.SYS (*/options*)

Use HIMEM.SYS to enable extended memory support for all DOS commands that make use of RAM above 1024Kb. Such CONFIG.SYS commands include EMM386.EXE, DOS=HIGH, as well as any device drive that is loaded into extended memory.

● OPTIONS

/A20CONTROL:[*ON/OFF*] Forces HIMEM.SYS to assume control of the *A20 interrupt handler* (that portion of memory used to access extended memory) at the time it is loaded, when set to ON. When set to OFF, HIMEM.SYS will assume control of the A20 interrupt handler only if it is not already being used when HIMEM.SYS is loaded.

/CPUCLOCK:[*ON/OFF*] When set to ON, slows down HIMEM.SYS on systems where the clock speed changes when HIMEM.SYS is loaded. Default is OFF.

/HMAMIN=*nn*

Specifies the amount of memory an application must use before having access to extended memory, where *nn* is the amount of memory in kilobytes. The valid range is 0–63Kb. Default is 0.

/INT15=*nnnn*

(HIMEM versions 2.7 and later) Specifies the starting address for extended memory support, where *nnnn* is a number representing the starting address in kilobytes. Allows HIMEM.SYS to ignore a portion of extended memory for use by programs that require extended memory but are not compatible with the XMS memory specification HIMEM.SYS uses.

/MACHINE:*aaaa*

Specifies the type of CPU that you are using to access the A20 interrupt handler. *Aaaa* can be either a character-based machine code or an equivalent number, as indicated in the following table:

Number	Machine Code	Description
1	AT	IBM PC/AT
2	PS2	IBM PS/2
3	PT1CASCADE	Phoenix Cascade BIOS
4	HPVECTRA	Hewlett-Packard Vectra A/A+
5	ATT6300PLUS	AT&T 6300+
6	ACER1100	Acer 1100
7	TOSHIBA	Toshiba 1600 and 1200XE
8	WYSE	Wyse 12.5Mhz 80286

Number	Machine Code	Description
9	TULIP	Tulip SX
10	ZENITH	Zenith ZBIOS
11	AT1	IBM PC/AT
12	CSS	CSS Labs
13	PHILIPS	Philips
14	FASTHP	Hewlett-Packard Vectra

/NUMHANDLES=*nnn*	Specifies how many memory block handles can be used simultaneously, where *nnn* is the number of handles. The valid range is 1–128 handles. Default is 32.
/SHADOWRAM:[*ON*/*OFF*]	Disables shadow RAM on some computers that support this feature, and adds the memory used by shadow RAM back to available memory, when set to OFF. When set to ON, HIMEM.SYS ignores shadow RAM. Default is OFF if your computer has less than 1Mb of extended memory.

• EXAMPLES

DEVICE=C:\DOS\HIMEM.SYS

enables XMS extended memory support for all available extended memory.

DEVICE=C:\DOS\HIMEM.SYS /INT15=2048

enables XMS extended memory support for all memory starting at 2048Kb, ignoring the extended memory from 1024Kb to 2048Kb so that it may be used by other programs not compatible with XMS.

• ERROR MESSAGES

Warning! Invalid parameter ignored

DOS cannot recognize a parameter you have entered on the HIMEM initialization line in CONFIG.SYS. Edit this line in the CONFIG.SYS file and reboot the computer.

• NOTES   Any DOS command that makes use of extended memory requires that HIMEM.SYS be loaded first. If you intend to use EMM386.SYS (or a compatible driver) to load support for expanded memory, you must load HIMEM.SYS first.

Do not load HIMEM.SYS with the DEVICEHIGH command. Use the DEVICE command instead.

PRINTER.SYS

3.3+

Loads international font sets for IBM printers.

• SYNTAX

DEVICE=(*drive:\path*) PRINTER.SYS LPT#=(type (,*code page,additional*))

To specify an international character set using the PRINTER.SYS driver, first indicate a parallel printer port (LPT1, 2, or 3), then indicate an IBM printer type and at least one character set code page. The *type* parameter is one of the following:

4201 or 4208	IBM Proprinter or fully compatible
5202	IBM Quietwriter III

The *code page* parameter is a three-digit number representing international character sets, as outlined in Table 2.1 in Part 2.

The *additional* parameter is a number indicating how many extra code pages you intend to prepare using the MODE command. Refer to the MODE command entry in Part 2 for details. Your system must be capable of handling multiple international character sets.

• EXAMPLES

DEVICE=C:\DOS\PRINTER.SYS LPT1=(4201,863,1)

loads the Canadian French printer font set for an IBM Proprinter (or fully compatible), and specifies that one additional font set will be prepared using the MODE command, in versions 4.0 and later. In versions 3.3 and earlier, use 002 as the code page to load the Canadian set.

• ERROR MESSAGES

Code page drive cannot be initialized

You may have included an invalid parameter in the PRINTER.SYS initialization line. Edit CONFIG.SYS and correct the syntax, then reboot the computer.

Invalid syntax on PRINTER.SYS code page

DOS does not understand the syntax you have entered on the PRINTER.SYS initialization line in CONFIG.SYS. Edit this line in the CONFIG.SYS file and reboot the computer. If you are using a word processor to edit the file, be sure to save it in ASCII format.

Unable to perform refresh operation

PRINTER.SYS cannot find the current code page in RAM. Prepare and select the code page using the MODE command, and configure PRINTER.SYS for buffers equal to or greater than 1.

• NOTES As an alternative to this driver, the COUNTRY.SYS and KEYBOARD.SYS files are also used to specify code page switching. COUNTRY.SYS is specified as a parameter to the NLSFUNC command; KEYBOARD.SYS is a parameter of the KEYB command that specifies several international keyboard layouts.

RAMDRIVE.SYS

3.0+

Initializes a RAM disk.

● SYNTAX

DEVICE=(*drive:\path*) RAMDRIVE.SYS *size sectors directory* (/E)

A RAM disk simulates a disk drive in RAM. RAM disks tend to be faster than physical drives, although the fastest hard disks can run almost as fast. RAM disks are also valuable when programs access the disk drive frequently, reducing drive wear as well as saving time.

RAM disks are volatile, however. You must save the data on a RAM disk to a physical drive before turning off the power to your computer. If you experience a power failure while running a RAM disk, all data that was not saved to a physical disk will be lost.

The *size* parameter indicates the storage area of the RAM disk, expressed in kilobytes. Default is 64, for 64Kb. The *sectors* parameter indicates the size of a disk sector, expressed in bytes. Default is 512 bytes. The *directory* parameter indicates the maximum number of directory entries, from 2 to 1024. Default is 64.

● OPTIONS

The following option switches place the RAM disk in either extended or expanded memory. Use one or the other, not both. If you do not include one of these switches DOS will place the RAM disk in conventional memory. If you install the RAM disk in extended memory using DOS version 4.0 or greater, load HIMEM.SYS first. If you install the disk in expanded memory, load a compatible expanded memory manager, such as EMM386.EXE, first.

/A   (Versions 5.0+) Stores the RAM disk in expanded memory.

/E   Stores the RAM disk in extended memory.

/X   Stores the RAM disk in expanded memory (earlier versions).

● EXAMPLES

DEVICE=C:\DOS\RAMDRIVE.SYS

installs a RAM disk with all default parameters. Disk size is 64Kb, sector size is 512 bytes, the maximum number of directory entries is 64, and the drive itself is located in conventional memory.

DEVICE=C:\DOS\RAMDRIVE.SYS 2048 512 1024 /E

installs a RAM disk in extended memory. Disk size is 2Mb (2048Kb); sector size is 512 bytes; maximum number of directory entries is 1024.

● ERROR MESSAGES

Bad extended memory manager control chain

The RAMDRIVE driver is in conflict with another driver in the CONFIG.SYS file. Remove all installable drivers that come before RAMDRIVE.SYS, except HIMEM.SYS, and re-install them one by one until the error message reappears. You must reboot your computer each time. Do not use the offending driver with RAMDRIVE.SYS.

Expanded memory manager not present

You must install the expanded memory manager before installing RAMDRIVE.SYS. Move the expanded memory manager initialization line to an earlier position in the CONFIG.SYS file.

Expanded memory status shows error

RAMDRIVE.SYS detected an error in your expanded memory manager. Consult the documentation for your expanded memory manager to solve the problem.

Extended memory manager not present

You must install the XMS extended memory manager HIMEM.SYS before installing RAMDRIVE.SYS. Move the HIMEM.SYS initialization line to an earlier position in the CONFIG.SYS file.

I/O error accessing drive memory

RAMDRIVE has discovered a RAM error while installing. Have the computer serviced.

No extended memory available

The XMS extended memory has been allocated to other applications and resident functions. Deactivate other drivers to make room for your RAM disk.

SETVER.EXE

5.0+

Installs a list of software applications that require DOS to supply an earlier version number.

● SYNTAX

DEVICE=<*drive:\path*> SETVER.EXE

The command to load the SETVER.EXE driver is automatically added to your CONFIG.SYS file when you install DOS 5.0. This command causes DOS to load a list of applications that require version numbers earlier than 5.0.

You can delete this command from your CONFIG.SYS file if you are sure that none of your applications require an earlier version number. If you want to view or modify the list of applications, refer to the SETVER command in Part 2.

SMARTDRV.SYS

4.0+

Installs an XMS-compatible disk cache.

● SYNTAX

DEVICE=(*drive:\path*) SMARTDRV.SYS *size* (/A)

A *disk cache* improves system performance by storing the locations of frequently accessed files in memory, thereby reducing the overall number of disk accesses.

SMARTDRV.SYS requires either extended or expanded memory. HIMEM.SYS must be loaded to use extended memory. Both HIMEM.SYS and EMM386.EXE (or a compatible expanded memory manager) must be loaded for SMARTDRV.SYS to use expanded memory.

The *size* parameter specifies the amount of memory to use for the disk cache, where *size* is a number indicating the amount of RAM in kilobytes; for example 512 equals 512Kb, not 512 bytes. If you are using extended memory, the default size is 256Kb; if you are using expanded memory, default is all of the expanded memory available.

• OPTIONS

/A   Instructs DOS to use expanded memory for the disk
      cache; requires expanded memory manager such as
      EMM386.EXE.

• EXAMPLES

DEVICE=C:\DOS\SMARTDRV.SYS

loads the disk cache using all default parameters: cache is in extended memory, using 256Kb.

DEVICE=C:\DOS\SMARTDRV.SYS 512 /A

loads the disk cache in expanded memory, using 512Kb.

• ERROR MESSAGES

Bad extended memory manager control chain

SMARTDRV.SYS is in conflict with another driver in the CON-
FIG.SYS file. Remove all installable drivers that come before
RAMDRIVE.SYS, except HIMEM.SYS, and re-install them one by
one until the error message reappears. You must reboot your
computer each time. Do not use the offending driver with
SMARTDRV.SYS.

Bad or missing SMARTDRV.SYS

DOS cannot locate the SMARTDRV.SYS driver, or the driver has become corrupted. Copy the driver file from backup onto the root
directory, or specify the location of the file on the initialization line
in CONFIG.SYS.

Error on extended memory allocation

SMARTDRV.SYS has discovered a RAM error while installing.
Consult the documentation for your expanded memory manager to
solve the problem. If necessary, have your computer serviced.

Expanded memory manager not present

You must install the expanded memory manager before installing SMARTDRV.SYS. Move the expanded memory manager initialization line to an earlier position in the CONFIG.SYS file.

Expanded memory status shows error

SMARTDRV.SYS detected an error in your expanded memory manager. Consult the documentation for your expanded memory manager to solve the problem.

Extended memory manager not present

You must install the XMS extended memory manager HIMEM.SYS before installing SMARTDRV.SYS. Move the HIMEM.SYS initialization line to an earlier position in the CONFIG.SYS file.

I/O error accessing cache memory

SMARTDRV.SYS has discovered a RAM error while installing. Have the computer serviced.

No extended memory available

The XMS extended memory has been allocated to other applications and resident functions. Deactivate other drivers to make room for your RAM disk.

No hard drives on system

You must install and format a hard-disk drive in order to use SMARTDRV.SYS.

Too many bytes per track on fixed drive

Your hard disk is a nonstandard type. SMARTDRV.SYS is not compatible; you cannot run this driver with your fixed disk.

● **NOTES**   If you are using both expanded and extended memory in your system, use extended memory for SMARTDRV.SYS.

Do not use SMARTDRV.SYS if you have other disk-caching schemes installed for your system, as these systems may conflict, causing loss of data.

Beware of using SMARTDRV.SYS if you are also using a third-party hard-disk manager program that revises the cylinder and sector information on a nonstandard hard disk. Some of these programs may conflict with SMARTDRV.SYS's caching scheme and destroy your partitioning information (along with all your data), causing the hard disk to crash. Instead, settle for the safer, low-performance option of increasing the number of buffers using the BUFFERS command.

Appendix D

General
DOS Error Messages

The error messages in this section apply to many DOS commands. Most are related to problems that might occur through incorrect syntax entry, hardware error, and memory conflict with other software, among other causes. The meaning of these messages is explained, followed by suggestions for solving the problem.

Not all error messages come from DOS; most applications have error messages of their own. If you receive an unfamiliar message while running an application, be sure to check the application's documentation for an explanation.

ABORT, RETRY, IGNORE, FAIL?

DOS failed to recognize an instruction it was given, or a disk or device error has prevented the instruction from being carried out. This message appears along with many of the other error messages in this appendix. You may choose one of 4 responses, as follows:

Abort   Press A to terminate the program entirely and return to the DOS prompt.

Retry   Press R to repeat the instruction. This works in cases where you can make a change in the system (for example, closing a disk-drive door), or when a momentary pause will allow a conflict to resolve itself (for example, waiting for the printer to warm up and come online). If you press R a few times and continue to receive this message, press A.

Ignore   Press I to continue with processing, as if the error had not occurred. This option is risky, and is not recommended unless you are a software developer testing a program, or are absolutely certain that continued processing will not have destructive results.

Fail   Press F to cancel the problematic instruction but continue with processing. Like Ignore, this is a risky option, because ignoring this instruction can cause unexpected results later on. Use it only if you know for certain what will happen.

ACCESS DENIED

You attempted to open a file that is either labelled read-only, stored on a write-protected disk, or locked on a network. This message also appears if you use the TYPE command on a subdirectory, or the CD or CHDIR command on a file. Use the ATTRIB command to remove the file's read-only status, remove the write protection from the disk, or change the file name specification, and then try again.

ARE YOU SURE?

You are about to delete all the files in the specified directory, or the currently logged directory. Enter Y if you intend to do this; otherwise, enter N.

BAD COMMAND OR FILE NAME

DOS did not recognize the command you entered at the DOS prompt. Check to make sure that you have entered the command correctly, and that the command file can be found either on the specified directory or on the search path indicated by the PATH command.

BAD OR MISSING COMMAND INTERPRETER

You have attempted to load a version of COMMAND.COM that is not compatible with the current operating system, or COM-MAND.COM cannot be found. Reboot, using a floppy if necessary. Check that the correct version of COMMAND.COM is on the root directory, and that the correct version of COMMAND.COM has been specified using the SHELL command in CONFIG.SYS.

BOOT ERROR

DOS was not able to detect the presence of the expected peripheral devices at boot time. Check your computer's setup parameters using your system's setup utility. If necessary, perform a low-level format and repartition the disk drive. If you cannot solve the problem yourself, have the computer serviced by a professional diagnostician.

CANNOT FIND SYSTEM FILES

You have attempted to load the operating system from a drive that does not contain system files. Copy the system files to the drive using the SYS command, and restore backup copies of CON-FIG.SYS and AUTOEXEC.BAT to the root directory if necessary. If you cannot restore the system files, boot from a floppy disk, backup your data, and reformat the disk using the FORMAT /S command.

CANNOT LOAD COMMAND, SYSTEM HALTED

An application has overwritten all or part of COMMAND.COM in memory, and DOS is unable to reload the command processor. Reboot the computer. Check the integrity of the data modified by the application. If necessary, copy COMMAND.COM to a directory where DOS can find it upon exiting the application.

CANNOT READ FILE ALLOCATION TABLE

The file allocation table has become corrupted. If you can still find some of your data, back up whatever you can find onto blank diskettes. Do not overwrite any previous backups. You may be able to repair the file allocation table using the CHKDSK command. If necessary, reformat the disk. If the problem occurs repeatedly, have the drive serviced or replaced.

CURRENT DRIVE IS NO LONGER VALID

The currently logged drive does not have a disk in it, the drive door is open, or the drive is unrecognizable on a network. Change to another drive with a disk in it. Insert a disk in the drive. Close the drive door.

DATA ERROR

DOS has detected inconsistencies in data while reading or writing a file. You are prompted to Abort or Retry the operation. Press R (Retry) a few times, but if the message persists, press A (Abort). Check the disk using the CHKDSK command. Make fresh backups of the data (do not overwrite current backups) and reformat the disk. If the problem persists or occurs on several disks, have the drive serviced.

ERROR IN EXE FILE

The application's executable file contains errors that interfere with processing. The file may be incompatible with your current version of DOS. Check for the correct DOS version; if the version is correct, copy a new executable file from backup copies or the master disk. If the problem persists, discard the executable files.

ERROR LOADING OPERATING SYSTEM

The operating system files cannot be found or have become corrupted. Copy the system files to the drive using the SYS command, and copy the CONFIG.SYS and AUTOEXEC.BAT files to the root directory if necessary. If you cannot restore the system files, boot from a floppy disk, back up your data, and reformat the disk using the FORMAT /S command.

ERROR READING DIRECTORY

The file allocation table or subdirectory structure has become corrupted. Back up whatever data that you can on blank diskettes; do not overwrite previous backups. Reformat the disk. If the problem persists, have the drive serviced.

ERROR READING SYSTEM FILE

See the "Error loading operating system" error message entry.

ERROR WRITING TO DEVICE

The peripheral device could not accept data being sent to it. Check that the device is on line, that the baud rate at which you are sending data is not too fast, and that the data being sent is appropriate for the device; for example, do not send data at 9600 baud if the device can only process 1200 baud, and do not send binary files to a device that can accept only ASCII files.

EXEC FAILURE

The application's executable file contains errors that interfere with processing, or the file cannot be opened because too many files are already open. The file may be incompatible with your current version of DOS. Check for the correct DOS version. If the DOS version is correct, copy a new executable file from backup copies or the master disk. Increase the number of open files by editing the FILES command in CONFIG.SYS, and rebooting the computer. If you determine that the executable file is damaged, discard it.

FILE ALLOCATION TABLE BAD

The file allocation table has become corrupted. Back up whatever data that you can on blank diskettes. Do not overwrite previous backups. You may solve the problem by invoking the CHKDSK command. If necessary, reformat the disk. If the problem repeats itself, have the drive serviced.

FILE CANNOT BE COPIED ONTO ITSELF

You have specified the same file as both the source and target. This often happens when wildcard characters have not been used carefully. Change the file specification for the source or target as necessary, and try again.

FILE CREATION ERROR

One of the following has happened:

- There was not enough space on the disk or chosen sub-directory for the file you tried to create.

- The file you tried to create already exists and is read-only.

- You tried to rename a file using a file name that already exists.

If the file is on the root directory, check that the maximum number of root directory files has not been reached. If the root directory (or entire disk) is full, delete some other files and try again. If the file in question is read-only, use a different target name, a different directory location, or use the ATTRIB command to remove the read-only attribute. You may be attempting to overwrite a hidden file; try a different target name or location. Also, if you are renaming files, use a different target name or location.

FILE NOT FOUND

The requested file was not found on the currently logged directory, or any of the directories specified with the PATH or APPEND commands. This message will also appear if the specified subdirectory is empty. Check the file name for correct spelling and correct location. If necessary, change the search path.

GENERAL FAILURE

The disk in the drive was not formatted, or formatted for a system other than DOS. Reformat the disk. If the problem continues, have the drive serviced.

INCORRECT DOS VERSION

You entered a DOS external command for a version that is different from the DOS version currently in RAM. Reboot with the correct version of DOS, or use the correct executable file for the command.

INCORRECT NUMBER OF PARAMETERS

See the "Invalid parameter" error message entry.

INSUFFICIENT DISK SPACE

You have used up all the available space on your disk for copying or creating files. Run CHKDSK to reclaim space that may be occupied by lost clusters. If necessary, delete some files.

INSUFFICIENT MEMORY

You do not have sufficient RAM to process the command you entered. Remove some memory-resident files. Reboot the computer if necessary. Add more RAM to your system to accommodate the application or command.

INTERMEDIATE FILE ERROR DURING PIPE

A temporary file, created during a piping operation, has become corrupted. The disk may be too full, too many files may be open, or a hardware problem has prevented successful processing. Run CHKDSK to determine if problems exist on the data drive. Delete unnecessary files to make room on the disk. Make sure the disk is not write-protected. If too many files were open, change the FILES command in CONFIG.SYS and reboot the computer.

INTERNAL ERROR

A memory conflict or other technical error has occurred. Reboot the computer. If you detect a pattern to the appearance of the error, restore the problem application or DOS file from backup, or re-install the file from master disks and try it again. If the message appears randomly, have the computer serviced by a qualified technician. Do not overwrite current backups with new backups after seeing this message until the cause is determined and the problem solved.

INVALID COMMAND.COM

See the "Bad or missing command interpreter" error message entry.

INVALID DIRECTORY

You have entered an invalid directory name or the name of a directory that does not exist, or DOS has discovered an invalid directory on the disk. Check the spelling of the directory name and reenter it if it is incorrect. If the invalid directory was discovered by DOS, back up what files you can onto fresh backup disks. Do not overwrite current backups. Reformat or replace the disk.

INVALID DISK CHANGE

DOS has discovered that you have changed disks during processing. Return the original disk to the drive. If disks have not been changed, this message may signal a hardware problem; have the drive serviced.

INVALID DRIVE SPECIFICATION

You have entered the letter of a drive that does not exist. Enter a different drive letter, or assign the drive letter using the ASSIGN or SUBST command.

INVALID FILENAME

You have entered a file name containing invalid or wildcard characters, or you have used a reserved device name as a file name. Try the command again using a different file specification.

INVALID FUNCTION PARAMETER

See the "Invalid parameter" error message entry.

INVALID KEYWORD

See the "Invalid parameter" error message entry.

INVALID PARAMETER

You have not specified the correct option switches on the command line, or have duplicated parameters, or have combined parameters illegally. Review the correct syntax of the command and try it again.

INVALID PARAMETER COMBINATION

See the "Invalid parameter" error message entry.

INVALID PARTITION TABLE

DOS has detected an error in the fixed disk's partition information. Back up whatever data you can, and run FDISK to initialize a valid partition table.

INVALID PATH

You have specified a nonexistent directory, or one that DOS cannot find. Check the drive and path specification, the spelling of the directory name, and the settings of the PATH and APPEND commands.

INVALID PATH, NOT DIRECTORY, OR DIRECTORY NOT EMPTY

DOS is not able to locate the specified directory, or you entered a file in place of a directory name, or the directory contains files (or other nested subdirectories) and cannot be removed. Check the spelling of the directory name, or list the contents of the directory. If it appears empty, it may contain hidden files. Use the DIR /A:H command to reveal any possibly hidden files.

INVALID SWITCH

See the "Invalid parameter" error message entry.

INVALID SYNTAX

DOS could not process the syntax you entered. Review the correct command syntax and try again.

MEMORY ALLOCATION ERROR

DOS was not able to configure RAM properly. Reboot the computer. If the problem does not go away, reboot from a floppy disk and copy new system files onto your hard disk. If the problem persists, have your computer's memory boards serviced.

MUST SPECIFY ON OR OFF

You have entered an invalid parameter for a command that requires either an ON or OFF parameter. Correct the syntax and reenter the command.

NO FIXED DISKS PRESENT

DOS was not able to detect the presence of a fixed disk drive. Check your computer's setup parameters for the correct drive type. If necessary, perform a low-level format and repartition the disk drive. If you cannot solve the problem yourself, have the computer serviced by a competent technician.

NO ROOM IN DIRECTORY

You have exceeded the limit on the number of allowable files in your root directory. Copy the file to a subdirectory or different disk.

NON-SYSTEM DISK OR DISK ERROR

DOS cannot find system files on the current disk. Insert a disk containing system files, or boot from the hard disk, if it contains system files.

NOT ENOUGH MEMORY

See the "Insufficient memory" error message entry.

OUT OF ENVIRONMENT SPACE

You have initialized too many operating system variables. Remove some variables using the SET command, or increase the size of the environment using the SHELL command in CONFIG.SYS, and reboot the computer.

PARAMETER FORMAT NOT CORRECT

See the "Invalid parameter" error message entry.

PARAMETER VALUE NOT ALLOWED

See the "Invalid parameter" error message entry.

PARAMETER VALUE NOT IN ALLOWED RANGE

See the "Invalid parameter" error message entry.

PARAMETERS NOT COMPATIBLE

See the "Invalid parameter" error message entry.

PARSE ERROR

You have entered a syntax error, but DOS cannot locate COM-MAND.COM to display a more precise error message. Reboot the computer if necessary; check the command syntax and try again.

PATH NOT FOUND

See the "Invalid path" error message entry.

PRINTER ERROR

DOS cannot send data to your printing device. Make sure the device is online, and that the output has not been redirected to a different port.

PROGRAM TOO BIG TO FIT IN MEMORY

See the "Insufficient memory" error message entry.

READ FAULT ERROR

DOS cannot read data on the disk. Re-insert the disk in the drive, and press R (Retry). If the error persists, run CHKDSK on the disk; if the disk is unrecoverable, reformat or discard it.

REQUIRED PARAMETER MISSING

See the "Invalid parameter" error message entry.

SAME PARAMETER ENTERED TWICE

See the "Invalid parameter" error message entry.

SECTOR NOT FOUND

DOS has discovered a formatting error on the disk. Run the RECOVER command on the desired file to move it to a stable area of the disk. Run CHKDSK to try to solve the disk's problems. If the problem persists, reformat or discard the disk.

SEEK ERROR

See the "Read fault error" error message entry.

SHARING VIOLATION

You have attempted to reopen or write to a file that is already open. This often occurs on a network, but may also occur on single-user systems with SHARE installed. Use your current application's commands to close the data file before attempting to reopen or write new data to it.

SPECIFIED COMMAND
SEARCH DIRECTORY BAD

The SHELL command in CONFIG.SYS contains invalid information. Edit this line in the CONFIG.SYS file, and reboot the computer.

SYNTAX ERROR

See the "Invalid parameter" error message entry.

TOO MANY FILES OPEN

See the "Too many open files" error message entry.

TOO MANY OPEN FILES

You have exceeded the maximum number of allowed open files on your system. Increase the maximum with the FILES command in CONFIG.SYS and reboot the computer.

TOO MANY PARAMETERS

See the "Invalid parameter" error message entry.

TOO MANY REDIRECTIONS

You have redirected data output to a device that does not exist, or have attempted to redirect data that has already been redirected. Correct the command line syntax for the correct device or a single redirection, and try again.

TOP LEVEL PROCESS
ABORTED, CANNOT CONTINUE

DOS was unable to return to the parent routine after completing a nested subroutine. Reboot the computer. Recopy the application files from backup or master disks. If using a batch file, edit the syntax for nested subroutines.

UNRECOGNIZED COMMAND IN CONFIG.SYS

DOS could not recognize a command in the CONFIG.SYS file when booting. Other messages that appear before this one may help you determine which lines are invalid. Edit CONFIG.SYS and correct the invalid lines. If you are editing CONFIG.SYS with a word processor, be sure that you save the file as an ASCII file.

UNRECOVERABLE READ OR WRITE ERROR

DOS could not read or write data to the disk. The disk is probably damaged. Use a different disk to save the current data. Run CHKDSK on the damaged disk to attempt to recover what files you can. Reformat the bad disk, or discard it.

WRITE FAULT ERROR

DOS cannot write data to the disk. Re-insert the disk in the drive, and press R (Retry). If the error persists, run CHKDSK on the disk; if the disk is unrecoverable, discard it.

WRITE PROTECT ERROR

DOS cannot write data to the disk because it is write-protected. Remove the write-protection tab from the disk, re-insert the disk in the drive, and press R (Retry). If the error persists, use a different disk.

Index

Q

R

S

Selections from The SYBEX Library

OPERATING SYSTEMS

The ABC's of DOS 4
Alan R. Miller
275pp. Ref. 583-2

This step-by-step introduction to using DOS 4 is written especially for beginners. Filled with simple examples, *The ABC's of DOS 4* covers the basics of hardware, software, disks, the system editor EDLIN, DOS commands, and more.

ABC's of MS-DOS (Second Edition)
Alan R. Miller
233pp. Ref. 493-3

This handy guide to MS-DOS is all many PC users need to manage their computer files, organize floppy and hard disks, use EDLIN, and keep their computers organized. Additional information is given about utilities like Sidekick, and there is a DOS command and program summary. The second edition is fully updated for Version 3.3.

DOS Assembly Language Programming
Alan R. Miller
365pp. 487-9

This book covers PC-DOS through 3.3, and gives clear explanations of how to assemble, link, and debug 8086, 8088, 80286, and 80386 programs. The example assembly language routines are valuable for students and programmers alike.

DOS 3.3 On-Line Advisor Version 1.1
SYBAR, Software Division of SYBEX, Inc.
Ref. 933-1

The answer to all your DOS problems. The DOS On-Line Advisor is an on-screen reference that explains over 200 DOS error messages. 2300 other citations cover all you ever needed to know about DOS. The DOS On-Line Advisor pops up on top of your working program to give you quick, easy help when you need it, and disappears when you don't. Covers thru version 3.3. Software package comes with 3½" and 5¼" disks. **System Requirements:** IBM compatible with DOS 2.0 or higher, runs with Windows 3.0, uses 90K of RAM.

DOS Instant Reference
SYBEX Prompter Series
Greg Harvey
Kay Yarborough Nelson
220pp. Ref. 477-1, 4 ¾" x 8"

A complete fingertip reference for fast, easy on-line help:command summaries, syntax, usage and error messages. Organized by function—system commands, file commands, disk management, directories, batch files, I/O, networking, programming, and more. Through Version 3.3.

Encyclopedia DOS
Judd Robbins
1030pp. Ref. 699-5

A comprehensive reference and user's guide to all versions of DOS through 4.0. Offers complete information on every DOS command, with all possible switches and parameters—plus examples of effective usage. An invaluable tool.

Essential OS/2 (Second Edition)
Judd Robbins
445pp. Ref. 609-X

Written by an OS/2 expert, this is the guide to the powerful new resources of the OS/2 operating system standard edition 1.1 with presentation manager. Robbins introduces the standard edition, and details multitasking under OS/2, and the range of commands for installing, starting up, configuring, and running applications. For Version 1.1 Standard Edition.

DOS Commands by Function

Function	Command to Use
Place comments in system or batch files	REM
Print a file from DOS	PRINT
Protect files on a network	SHARE
Recover an accidentally erased file	UNDELETE
Recover from an accidental disk format	MIRROR, UNFORMAT
Redirect parallel output to serial	MODE
Remove an empty subdirectory	RD, RMDIR
Remove bad disk sectors	RECOVER
Repeat commands in a batch file	FOR, GOTO
Restore data from backups	COPY, REPLACE, RESTORE, XCOPY
Run a subroutine in a batch file	CALL
Send graphics characters to the printer	GRAPHICS
Send screen output to a remote terminal	CTTY
Set a new screen length or width	MODE
Set the time	TIME
Shift the screen display right or left	MODE
Skip lines in a batch file	GOTO